'This comprehensive text will inspire and support the development of effective leadership of self, others and organisations. Through clearly presented theory and engaging case studies, these skilled and experienced practitioners demonstrate the power of the Functional Fluency approach, illuminating the what, why and how of effective leadership in our increasingly complex and demanding world.'

Graeme Summers, *London Business School Executive Coach and co-author of* Co-creative Transactional Analysis

T0292826

The Fluent Leader

In this insightful and comprehensive volume, leaders and managers can explore how they can use their power and choice of behavioural options more effectively to develop a positive and healthy working environment where people and the organization can succeed.

Based on the Functional Fluency model as it was created by Dr Susannah Temple, this book details the art and skill of interpersonal effectiveness, describing the behaviours that enable human beings to get along well together and to flourish and thrive. Fluent leaders make positive and flexible responses which help things turn out well, instead of repeating old automatic reactions that sometimes make things worse. By inspiring and motivating others, they manage and lead constructively, saving time, energy, and stress. Further, becoming functionally fluent will improve their problem-solving, decision-making, and communication skills, enabling them to cultivate successful relationships. Through engaging case studies and opportunities for personal reflection, *The Fluent Leader* addresses situations leaders face as managers, team leaders, senior executives, and change agents.

The Fluent Leader guides leaders and managers, at all levels in any kind of organization, in how to use the most effective behaviours, and how to change ineffective behaviours, which are draining them or holding them back.

Valerie Fawcett is a learning and development specialist and a provider of training in Functional Fluency and the accompanying TIFF© (Temple Index of Functional Fluency) behavioural profile. She teaches and coaches groups and individuals in leadership and management.

The Fluent Leader

Functional Fluency and Effective Leadership Inspired by Transactional Analysis

Edited by Valerie Fawcett

Routledge
Taylor & Francis Group

LONDON AND NEW YORK

Designed cover image: Cover image and illustrations by Ivonne Zegveld

First published 2023
by Routledge
4 Park Square, Milton Park, Abingdon, Oxon OX14 4RN

and by Routledge
605 Third Avenue, New York, NY 10158

Routledge is an imprint of the Taylor & Francis Group, an informa business

British Library Cataloguing-in-Publication Data
A catalogue record for this book is available from the British Library

Library of Congress Cataloging-in-Publication Data
Names: Fawcett, Valerie, 1954- editor.
Title: The fluent leader : functional fluency and effective leadership inspired by transactional analysis / edited by Valerie Fawcett.
Description: New York, NY : Routledge, 2023. | Includes bibliographical references and index.
Identifiers: LCCN 2022048828 (print) | LCCN 2022048829 (ebook) | ISBN 9781032385402 (trade paperback) | ISBN 9781032385419 (hardback) | ISBN 9781003345527 (ebook)
Subjects: LCSH: Leadership--Psychological aspects. | Organizational change. | Organizational effectiveness.
Classification: LCC BF637.L4 .F588 2023 (print) | LCC BF637.L4 (ebook) | DDC 158/.4--dc23/eng/20221128
LC record available at https://lccn.loc.gov/2022048828
LC ebook record available at https://lccn.loc.gov/2022048829

ISBN: 978-1-032-38541-9 (hbk)
ISBN: 978-1-032-38540-2 (pbk)
ISBN: 978-1-003-34552-7 (ebk)

DOI: 10.4324/9781003345527

Contents

Figures

Contributors

Leona Bishop, Managing Director, Functional Fluency International, The Netherlands. Leona specializes in leadership, team, and organizational development. She has 20-plus years of experience working with individuals, teams, and organizations (public and private sector). She is a certified coach, an advanced trainee in Transactional Analysis, and a Licensed TIFF © Provider.

Martin van den Blink, Director/owner, Balance Consultancy Group, Curaçao. Martin is an organizational consultant and coach. He lives on Curaçao and works on several islands in the Caribbean. As an experienced team coach, he supports teams in gaining insight into their qualities, and stimulates team members to work together effectively, complementing each other's talents.

David Scott Brown, Coach, Trainer and Director at Future Fixers CIC, United Kingdom David is an experienced educator, coach, and trainer. His key interests are in learning and in empowering people to address climate change. He works with a wide range of clients, including teachers and head teachers, leaders in the not-for-profit sector, and entrepreneurs establishing people and planet-focused businesses.

Valerie Fawcett, Coach, Trainer and Mediator, Valerie Fawcett Associates, United Kingdom. Valerie provides coaching, training, and workplace mediation for leaders and managers in organizations of all types. She is also an Associate Lecturer in Psychology with The Open University.

Stefan F. Graebe, Founder/owner, My Wings Coaching, South Africa. Combining years of personal executive management experience with over a decade of coaching the realities of personal and professional issues, Stefan creates space and stimulation for leaders to reflect and grow. Stefan's client base includes private individuals as well as businesses and NGOs ranging from small to large and from start-up to mature.

Jutta Kreyenberg, Freelancer and Associate with Professio, Germany. Jutta is a psychologist, executive coach, and team trainer.

Paul Robinson, Managing Director, Quay Interactions Ltd., United Kingdom. Paul has been supporting people and organizations to learn and develop for 30 years as a manager, mentor, consultant, and trainer. He uses co-creative transactional analysis as a base for his work and is an Educational Transactional Analyst (PTSTA-E). He is based in Ipswich (UK) and delivers programmes internationally.

Rona Rowe, Independent Leadership Coach and Trainer, United Kingdom. Rona is trained in Transactional Analysis and works as a leadership coach and learning consultant, mainly with public service clients in the UK.

Hannah Titilayo Seriki, Operations Director, Functional Fluency International, South Africa. Layo's work as a Researcher, Coach, and Consultant concentrates on identifying what is needed to optimise people's effectiveness and contentedness. Transactional Analysis and Systemic Constellations are important modalities contributing to her development. She works with clients one-on-one and in groups, in various spaces – from offices to horse paddocks.

Acknowledgements

The editor of *The Fluent Leader* would like to acknowledge the help of many colleagues in the Functional Fluency International network, and others outside the network in organizations around the world, who have helped to review and shape this book.

We are grateful to the following for permission to reproduce copyright material:

Dr. Susannah Temple for permission to reproduce *The Power of Choice* diagram

The Chartered Institute of Personnel and Development in London (www. cipd.co.uk) for permission to include *Managing for sustainable engagement framework* from their report *Managing for sustainable employee engagement: guidance for employers and managers* [online]. Available at https://www.cipd. co.uk/knowledge/fundamentals/relations/engagement/management-guide

Taylor and Francis Group, LLC, a division of Informa plc. for permission to reproduce Blake Mouton Managerial Grid, Copyright 1991, from *Leadership Dilemmas-Grid Solutions* by Blake, Robert R., McCanse, Anne E.

Preface

The inspiration for this book comes from the work my colleagues and I do with individuals and groups in organizations. As coaches, trainers, and consultants, drawing on a variety of theories and models of leadership and management, we have in common our appreciation of the value provided to our clients by the Functional Fluency model of effective and ineffective behaviours created by Dr Susannah Temple. We wrote this book together to provide more leaders and managers, and those aspiring to those roles, with access to the learning and insights we know can come from Functional Fluency. Other coaches and trainers will also find it helpful.

Susannah Temple is an inspiring teacher who has had a long and successful career as a teacher, counsellor, and supervisor of both young people and other teachers, and as a writer and teacher of Transactional Analysis, the psychology originated by Eric Berne. She was awarded the Eric Berne Memorial Award from the International Transactional Analysis Association in 2014 for her work in developing Functional Fluency and the TIFF personal profiling tool based on it (see the Appendix).

Eric Berne was the author of *Games People Play,* and other books derived from his experience of the people he worked with. Others all over the world have taken up his ideas and run with them, developing TA into one of the most widely respected psychological guides to understanding human feelings, thoughts, attitudes, and behaviours. In researching and developing Functional Fluency, Susannah built on this work too, but a knowledge of TA is not required to benefit from her explanation of the behaviours human beings use when they have flourishing, constructive relationships with themselves and others, and the behaviours which hold them back or cause conflict.

Susannah's work, and ours, is now the basis for an international network of trainers and coaches, Functional Fluency International. The Appendix to this book contains more information about the training, resources, and information available to everyone through FFI.

Whether you are a leader, manager, coach or anyone else interested in promoting effective leadership in organizations, we hope you will find this book inspiring and helpful.

Valerie Fawcett

Chapter 1

Leadership, Fluency, and Where to Invest It

Stefan F. Graebe

"Functional what?" – a preamble

By the time I first came into contact with "Functional Fluency", I had been in executive leadership positions and associated training for over a decade. On being invited for an introductory training session, this is what caught me off-guard:

*   How powerful it is, whilst being intuitively accessible
*   How generally applicable it is

But what stunned me was simply:

*   I had never heard of it!

"Functional what?" was my first thought.

Yet, only a few hours later I wished I had known about it throughout my career. I had been in positions ranging from technical geek expert, to project leader, head of department, chief strategist, and CEO. To my surprise, I recall thinking that an understanding of Functional Fluency would have been highly relevant and helpful in each and every one of those positions.

It is equally applicable across a variety of sectors, such as private and public corporate sector, governments, NGOs, communities, hospitality, and leisure. The take-away point is that no matter a leader's level of seniority and no matter their sector of activity, the keys and principles of Functional Fluency will be any leader's good friend in everyday life and crisis alike.

The aim of this book is to share the power of Functional Fluency on a broader basis than we, the authors of this book, could reach in our face-to-face contacts. So, if you are involved with leadership and your first thought upon hearing Functional Fluency is, "Functional what?", then this book is for you.

DOI: 10.4324/9781003345527-1

In a nutshell: two keys and a principle

Essentially, Functional Fluency (FF) is about two keys and one principle. The two keys are:

- How to build effective relationships, understanding the what and how
- How to respond deliberately rather than react habitually

The principle is to use these keys with fluency, rather than in a rigid, recipe-like procedure. More will be said about this by the end of the chapter.

Sources of leadership challenges

Broadly speaking, leadership challenges arise from three sources:

- The nature of the leadership role:
  e.g. sailing if you are a yacht captain, cooking if a chef, medical if a doctor, financial if a CEO of a company
- Sources outside the leader:
  e.g. the market, changing laws, technology, pandemics, staff, competitors
- Sources within the leader:
  e.g. attitudes, beliefs, habits, socialization

I could repeat the list with these additional, somewhat challenging, comments:

- The nature of the leadership role: usually the focus of training, and regulated
- Sources outside the leader: often feared and bemoaned
- Sources within the leader: often unexplored yet habitually reacted on

There are, of course, common support-structures available to leaders to address these challenges. The first type of challenge is often well covered by the leader's studies, qualifications, up-skilling, and on-the-job training providing experience.

- Challenges from market and other external conditions can be addressed with colleagues, boards, consultants, and associations
- Challenges from within the leader can be explored with coaches, mentors and therapists, but this only happens if the leader seeks the support

All of these systems play important roles and continue to be optimized and updated. Their weakspot is, however, when leadership challenges arise from all sources at the same time and they start interacting.

This might sound a bit theoretical, but it is actually very common, as the following example illustrates.

Case Study: Captain Frederic on the Yacht

Frederic is the captain of a two-person yacht sailing in the national competition that they both long to win. Years of training, time, and sacrifice are on the line.

Suddenly, the weather conditions change (a challenge with source outside the leader). Frederic draws on his sailing knowledge (drawing on his training preparing him for the nature of his leadership role) and he starts weighing up two options. He feels exhilarated by the situation, relishing the forces of nature, his leadership role and the spirit of competition.

Just then, his crew mate calls out, somewhat arrogantly pointing to one of the two options as being obviously the best course of action.

Something in Frederic is triggered. He is not actually thinking of his older brother that always put him down and teased him that he didn't have a captain's grit. He's not actively thinking about those memories, but it does feel familiar, and the reactions seem automatic. Frederic's thinking and weighing up of options shuts down, squeezed into a dark narrow funnel that seems to allow but one decision: assert your leadership, do not choose the crew mate's recommendation, decide on the other one.

In this example, all three sources of leadership challenges come together and interact:

- Making the correct sailing decision is a challenge arising from this particular leadership role (yacht captain)
- The changed weather is a challenge arising from outside the leader
- The emotions triggered by the crew mate are a challenge from inside the leader

Frederic succumbs to his internal challenge, and lets it impact on his decision-making and leadership. These kinds of interactions between challenges are not easily detected by the support systems mentioned above because they largely treat the challenges separately.

Whilst it is safe to say that every person will have detected and dealt with some of their internal challenges in the course of life, it is the ones that we are unaware of that can limit the effectiveness of our leadership. And the longer they remain undetected to the leader, the more habituated the reactions become; they then seem inevitable and automatic, limiting the leader's choice of response. This is addressed by the first key of Functional Fluency.

FF Key 1: Responding deliberately rather than reacting habitually

The first key that Functional Fluency alerts leaders to is practising one's ability to respond instead of react. The crucial difference between the two is this. Reacting is what is colloquially also known as a knee-jerk reaction. It feels as if the reaction is inevitable, as if there were no other alternative.

In contrast, responding involves a sense of choice in which the person deliberately picks the behaviour most effective in the situation.

Reactions often stem from a time when we deemed them a good or only option (frequently in early life or early in a new role) and then they become habit over the years. Eventually they are near automatic and appear to be without viable alternative.

Examples include someone with a tendency to behave like a victim, or someone with a vicious temper, aggression, submission, smothering and the like.

Case Study: Thomas and his temper

Thomas has a temper; he has had it as long as he can remember and has often been disciplined for it, particularly as a child. But he has become used to the consequences; he feels it works for him, and he carries it like a badge of honour.

Almost every time a team member in the IT group that he manages has an idea other than his own, Thomas feels challenged and reacts to the perceived attack by shutting it down angrily. The words to emphasize in this sentence are "almost every time". That makes it a reaction that feels automatic and inevitable.

When Thomas is exposed to a Functional Fluency leadership course, he becomes aware of his limiting habit. During the training, he practises possible alternative behaviours when he feels challenged; for example, listening, questioning, understanding, discussing and collaborating to find a great idea that he and the entire team own and believe in.

Once Thomas has mastered considering more options of behaviour, he has discovered his capacity to respond by choosing an effective behaviour rather than reacting out of habitual reflex. At first, responding deliberately rather than reacting "automatically" can be difficult with long-standing habits and emotional triggers.

But it is like writing with your non-writing hand: in the beginning it is awkward, unfamiliar and inefficient. But if you were forced to do so because, say, you had your writing hand in a cast, you would eventually get ever more skilled at it. Indeed, if the cast came off after a sufficiently long time, writing with your former writing hand would suddenly be the unfamiliar experience.

Thus, what is often said about habits, namely "use them or lose them", can be enlisted to work in your favour: practise a more effective behaviour instead of a less effective one. The more you use the effective one, the more you will lose the less effective other - double whammy - that is how habits work.

Similarly to the handwriting example, in the heat of the moment Thomas might initially fall back into his habit of shutting down his team's ideas. But after a while, he will be able to realize it in hindsight and will be able to come up with alternative behaviour that could have been more effective.

Eventually he will be able to do it in real time provided the situation is not too stressful. And with yet more awareness and practice he will master responding on his toes in stressful situations. That is when Thomas will have gained fluency at this skill.

FF Key 2: Building effective relationships

The second key that Functional Fluency offers leaders is how to build and maintain effective relationships.

"Effective" is defined as something that is successful at producing a desired result. So, whilst mutual respect, caring and having fun all contribute towards effectiveness, the important attribute of an effective relationship is that the relationship itself is a key success factor in achieving the goal.

The Big Five of FF: Effectiveness in four elements of behaviour plus awareness

The research at the basis of FF has found that the myriads of subtleties in a relationship can broadly be looked at in terms of four Elements in which your behaviour can be effective or not (Figure 1.1).

1   How you "Guide and Direct Others and Yourself"
2   How you "Look after Others and Yourself"
In acting on behalf of yourself:
3   How you inject yourself into the relationship by "Expressing Your Own Self"
4   How you liaise and co-operate by "Relating to Others"

Figure 1.1 Four Elements of Effective Relationships.

Figure 1.2 Effective and Ineffective Behaviours in Relationships.

Each of these four Elements can then be further divided into a spectrum that spans from effective to ineffective behaviours as exemplified in Figure 1.2.

The more a leader can spend time and energy in effective behaviours, and the more the leader can solicit effective responses from everybody they are interacting with, the more their relationships become effective relationships.

This, now, gives a new significance to the first key (responding deliberately rather than reacting habitually) as, inevitably, most people will have made some ineffective behaviour a habit. Usually, it would not be that a person always expressed that behaviour; more likely it is because a particular topic, a particular person, a tone of voice or something of this nature triggers an ineffective behaviour.

The journey to becoming a more effective leader is to first become aware of the triggers and patterns. Subsequently, one can then practise breaking the ineffective habit and responding deliberately with more effective behaviour.

To complete the picture, one more Element is needed: the skill of situational awareness.

What use is it, when a leader has a great toolbox of effective behaviours at their disposal if they habitually read the situation incorrectly? If, for example, someone was very effective at responding to rebellion, but

Figure 1.3 The Big Five Elements of Functional Fluency.

continuously misread situations as being rebellions against them rather than a team offering their cooperation?

Therefore, the central Element of the FF Big Five is the ability to read the situation. It is situational awareness, the reading of "what is going on inside me and outside me." This is summarized by the term Accounting (Figure 1.3).

Why Functional Fluency is so widely applicable

Being *capable* of something is one thing, being *fluent* at it is that special extra. Being capable of reading words is one thing, telling a story fluently, so that it captivates and galvanizes an audience is that special something.

As an established or aspiring leader, you will need to cultivate and draw on many capabilities. You need whatever is required for your portfolio; you need experience, support and connectivity; you need to be highly capable of communicating, networking, and any number of other skills.

But let us return to the difference between being capable versus the additional special extra of being fluent, galvanizing, visionary, creating leadership, where people feel they can be and want to be and become and belong. Considering all of these demands, where would you choose to become fluent beyond just being capable?

Becoming fluent in building effective relationships and responding deliberately is a great investment. Here are some reasons, in no particular order.

Wherever you are, whatever the times

No matter what your present position is, junior, senior, expert, general: there is no doubt that you will be more effective if you have more effective relationships. Being networked itself says nothing about the quality of the network. Effective relationships do.

As you grow and mature

However you grow: whether you acquire decades of experience and expertise or acquire broad competency, whether you get thrust into the deep end or thrust yourself into the deep end, or walk to wherever you feel fulfilled you will need *capability*. But being *fluent* at building effective relationships will support you in finding what fulfils you most personally.

Turning uncertainty into excitement

"Best practice" has been the compass telling us how to do things. It is based on predictability. The hallmark of our times, however, has been uncertainty, unpredictability and disruption of what was, just yesterday, "Best Practice". When worlds change and Best Practice breaks down, it never breaks down completely. Your effective relationships will adapt and support managing the uncertain or unknown, and that can become quite exciting.

Nature, nurture, future

There has been much research and an intricate debate headlined by the catchy phrase "Nature versus Nurture". It essentially asks whether we are more impacted by what we are born with (genes, biology, chemistry, and evolution) or by how we grow up individually (childhood, socialization, education, and personal history).

Research acknowledges that both play a role; it is the degree and the scope of our everyday human experience that are most debated and how exactly "Nature" and "Nurture" affect each other. There are also overlapping questions such as the extent to which personality is either more intrinsic (nature) or more habitual (nurture).

Functional Fluency invites you on a journey that has space for either but shifts the emphasis onto a third "-*ture*": your Future and its possibilities. In "Nature, Nurture, Future" the first word derives from the Latin *nat-* (meaning born, birth), the second from *nutrire* (nourish, feed, cherish) and the third one from futures (meaning grow, become). The ending –*ture* makes each word a noun.

So these three words represent your nature and inclinations, the socialization, thoughts and behaviours you have habituated, and finally the directions in which you might develop more effective behaviours and relationships.

When you start using aspects of Functional Fluency you have not used before, you will alternate between contemplating your current behavioural tendencies, triggers and consequences, and exploring possible alternatives. We hope that you will enjoy the journey!

Summary: 3 challenges, 2 keys, I principle

This chapter can be concisely summarized with the memory hook "3, 2, 1":

There are:

- 3 sources of leadership challenges – nature of portfolio, external, and internal for which Functional Fluency offers
- 2 keys – responding instead of reacting to build effective relationships
- 1 principle – becoming fluent at using the keys

Chapter-by-chapter guide

We recommend that you read the first four chapters in order. After that, you may wish to choose the topics which most interest you, but we believe that reading all chapters provides the best understanding of functionally fluent behaviour with others and yourself. All chapters include examples and case studies to illustrate the topic, and short reflective exercises to help you to relate your reading to your own situation, and direct your energy into more effective behaviours.

Chapter 2 What is Functional Fluency? A Guide to Effective Behaviours. This is the practical guide to the Functional Fluency model, describing the behavioural styles in detail, and providing practical examples of their use in management and leadership situations. It is intended that readers will return to this guide as they need to while reading the rest of the book.

Chapter 3 The Constructive Manager – Building Effective Relationships. The focus in this chapter is on using functionally fluent behaviours as a first line leader, including those new to management, in order to have constructive relationships with your team. It provides examples and case studies to illustrate sections on Understanding your role, "Rookie" mistakes, Managing performance and the wider perspective of management and leadership.

Chapter 4 The Inspirational Leader – Sharing Vision and Purpose. Picking up from Chapter 3, this chapter considers the behaviours needed by those who move into middle and senior management roles. It explores how Functional Fluency can help senior leaders with the key challenges of their roles, such as VUCA, shared and transformational leadership, and strategic thinking and communication.

Chapter 5 Building your Personal Resilience with Functional Fluency. Most of the chapters show how functionally fluent behaviour applies to relationships with both others and yourself, but this chapter focuses on how we can take responsibility for ourselves either in ways which increase our personal resilience and well-being, or undermine it.

Chapter 6 Fluent Teamwork – Effective Interaction through Conscious Choices. Teams which work together well are generally using functionally fluent behaviours. This chapter describes how, as well as what happens when team members fall into ineffective behaviours. The part played by the functionally fluent team leader is illustrated by examples.

Chapter 7 Embracing challenging relationships for effective leadership: three perspectives. This chapter encourages leaders to embrace interpersonal challenges on their way to evolving their leadership by looking at the individual, group, and organizational aspects of working relationships. It explores the necessary conditions to develop trust and psychological safety in order to create a new functional reality through an extended case study.

Chapter 8 Using Functional Fluency to support Organizational Development and Transformational Change. Functional Fluency provides guidance for constructive development and change throughout a whole department or organization, not just the individuals. This chapter shows how the behaviours can guide a successful change programme both for the change leaders and those experiencing the change and provides an extended case study of a change led by the author.

Appendix: Functional Fluency Courses and the TIFF Personal Profiling tool. The authors of this book and their colleagues come from an international network (Functional Fluency International) which provides consultancy, coaching, and training in Functional Fluency, and the accompanying behavioural profile (TIFF) for individuals and teams.

The case studies in the book come from real coaching carried out by the chapter authors, and in some cases this has included personal profiling for the individual in Functional Fluency behaviours. The profiling tool, TIFF or Temple Index of Functional Fluency, is named after the developer of Functional Fluency. There is more about Susannah Temple and her research in the Preface (in case you missed it!). The Appendix provides further information about the learning which is available to help you take your use of Functional Fluency further, including TIFF profiling and free resources, and how to get in touch with the authors and other TIFF and Functional Fluency trainers, coaches, and consultants.

Chapter 2

What Is Functional Fluency? A Guide to Effective Behaviours

Valerie Fawcett and Stefan F. Graebe

What is Functional Fluency?

In Chapter 1 you were introduced to four behavioural categories which provide the keys to using effective behaviours instead of ineffective, and to putting energy into responses rather than reactions. To these were added the Accounting behaviour which enables us to use situational awareness to choose the behaviour we use. Where do these categories come from? What do we mean by Functional Fluency? This chapter provides the guide to how you can direct your energy into the behaviours which will make you more effective in your role as a leader and manager and in other areas of your life as well. Reading this chapter (and flipping back to it when you need to) will help you get the most from the other chapters in this book.

Functional Fluency is the art and skill of effective relationships, a way of looking at effective behaviours in flourishing relationships of all kinds, including leadership and management. It was researched by Susannah Temple (see the Preface and Appendix for more on this research).

Most people in management and leadership roles are putting large amounts of energy into the work they do, and the relationships they have with staff and work colleagues. The Power of Choice diagram (Figure 2.1) shows how any event or situation invokes behaviour from thoughts and feelings. A successful outcome involves making a choice before acting.

Functionally fluent behaviour is all about using your energy to do what works and leads to success and fulfilment. A good question to ask yourself is "Who benefits if I do this?" If the answer is "No-one" or "Only me" or, in some cases, "Only someone else", you could probably make a better choice. How much of your energy is wasted in the use of ineffective behaviours? How can you make some changes which will give you better working relationships and greater success in your working life and personal life?

Here's how it works.

DOI: 10.4324/9781003345527-2

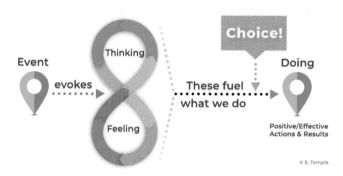

Figure 2.1 The Power of Choice.[1]

The levels of behaviour

Level 1

At the basic level, we use our behaviour in three ways. As individuals, we use our behaviour on behalf of ourselves and have done ever since we were children, changing that behaviour as we grew up and developed as adults, but still revisiting old behaviours. In Figure 2.2, we are calling that Being an Individual.

As we grew up, we took on roles of responsibility for ourselves and for others, from caring for a sibling or parent, or becoming captain of a sports team, to being a parent and/or becoming a leader or manager of others in a work role. Some of these represent appointed or long-standing roles and others temporary, such as taking the lead amongst a group of friends or colleagues.

In Figure 2.2, we are calling that Being in Charge.

The third way we use our behaviour is Accounting - the situational awareness referred to in Chapter 1. This is mostly going on in our own heads but may involve enquiring from others what is going on for them. It is about noticing and evaluating reality in any situation, inside ourselves and others, checking things out, thinking with emotional intelligence, and rationalizing about consequences and needs. When we are assessing reality effectively, we are using "head, heart and guts". Clear and informed thinking about reality enables us to use other effective behaviours.

Level 2

Accounting remains at Level 2 as one of five elements of behaviour. As shown in Figure 2.2, the Being-in-Charge and Being-an-Individual groups of

Figure 2.2 Five Elements of Behaviour.

behaviours are each divided into two, and this provides the other four elements you were introduced to in the first chapter:

Being in Charge

- Guiding and Directing others and yourself
- Looking After others and yourself

Being an Individual

- Expressing My Own Self
- Relating to Others

Each of these can be done either effectively and constructively, or ineffectively and with the possibility of upset or conflict. Accounting is a contributor to the effective behaviours. It is impossible to be effective if you do not have situational awareness or are making assumptions or entertaining fantasies which cloud the picture.

Reflection

Before you read on, think about some interactions you have had with others in recent days. They can be situations in your role as a leader of yourself or others, or as an individual acting on your own behalf. Think of one which

DOMINATING
bossy
fault-finding
punitive

inspiring
well-organised
firm
STRUCTURING

Guiding
and
directing

alert
aware

ACCOU
Assessing
outer curre

COOPERATIVE
friendly
assertive
considerate

anxious · rebellious
submissive
**COMPLIANT
RESISTANT**

Relating
to
others

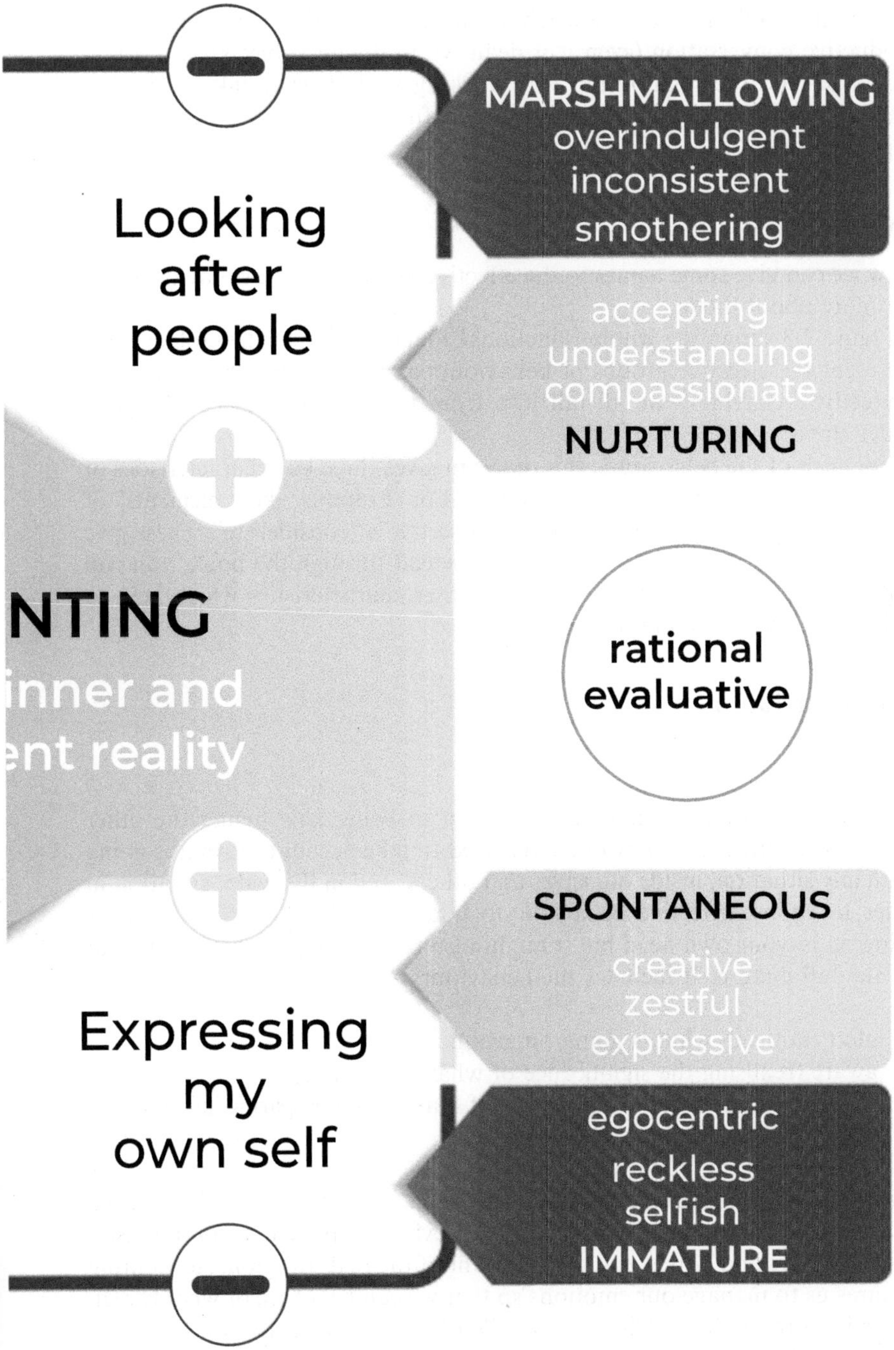

Looking after people

MARSHMALLOWING
overindulgent
inconsistent
smothering

accepting
understanding
compassionate
NURTURING

NTING
inner and
ent reality

rational
evaluative

SPONTANEOUS
creative
zestful
expressive

Expressing my own self

egocentric
reckless
selfish
IMMATURE

Figure 2.3 The Complete Functional Fluency model.

went really well and you were left feeling you'd had a constructive and productive conversation (even if it dealt with difficult subjects) or a joyful exchange, and the relationship was working well. Then think of another which left you feeling upset, angry or confused, or even puzzled; "What happened there?!".

Level 3

Now we can give some names to the effective and ineffective behaviours and say more about them.

Figure 2.3 shows the whole Functional Fluency model. The Golden Five represent the effective groups of behaviours and the Purple Pitfalls are the ineffective behaviours we all fall into from time to time, especially when under stress.

For each of the behaviours, this diagram gives three key characteristics of the behaviour (four for Accounting). For example, key elements of Cooperative behaviour are "friendly", "assertive", "considerate". These give you a snapshot of the behaviours. As you read through the book, you will find that we provide more detail and further characteristics which help to explain the behaviours in more depth.

The behaviours

Accounting

Accounting in Functional Fluency is vital to being able to use the other Golden Five effective behaviours. We need to take account of what is going on in any situation, inside ourselves and others, and in the wider situation in order to choose effective behaviour to address it. Mostly, Accounting is going on in your own head but it might also require enquiry from others to get the full picture. It includes the behaviours:

alert (noticing what is going on around you)
aware (realising the significance of what you notice)
evaluative (assessing the importance of something, comparing information)
rational (thinking logically, using facts)

When our emotions are hooked in a situation, it can be hard to leave aside assumptions based on our beliefs and previous experiences, or fantasies based on fears and hopes, and take account of the real situation. Accounting requires us to manage our emotions so that we can be aware of what is real. There is more on this in Chapter 5 on *Building your Personal Resilience with Functional Fluency*.

Case study

Donna is full of enthusiasm for a plan she has to reorganize her department and introduce a new procedure which she is sure will cut staff workload and enable the team to be more productive. She is relatively new to the company and was appointed, she was told, because of her contribution in a competitor company which was very successful. Donna thought that she would be able to simply propose the changes and be given permission by her senior managers to go ahead. However, she is surprised to find that the senior management team is reluctant to just accept her recommendations. In working with a coach on her Functional Fluency, Donna realizes that the company she is now working for has previously made changes which have caused the company significant losses. In Accounting for this situation, Donna realizes that her own enthusiasm is not enough here. She needs to find out more about how other departments might react to her proposals, and address any concerns in how she presents the changes to senior managers. She then needs to plan a step-by-step approach which will bring people on board with her ideas, and ensure that she is clear how to tailor them to the needs of this organization.

Guiding and directing – Structuring or Dominating

These Being-in-Charge behaviours refer particularly to your role as a leader, manager of others or whenever you are the one who takes the lead because of your greater knowledge or skill, or the need at the time, so it can refer to ad hoc situations, project management or team working. It also refers to your role as a parent if you have children, so you may like to reflect on those relationships as well. One side refers to the "control" aspect of your social responsibility in this role (Guiding and Directing) and the other side to the "care" aspect (Looking after People).

When guiding and directing others, studies have shown that Structuring behaviours such as

- inspiring (exciting someone through your own example or enthusiasm)
- well-organized (showing effective organization to benefit self and others)
- firm (being steadfast and setting boundaries where necessary)

are generally more effective than Dominating behaviours

- bossy (giving orders excessively)
- fault-finding (quickly pointing out mistakes and ignoring successes)
- punitive (inflicting a punishment on self or others)

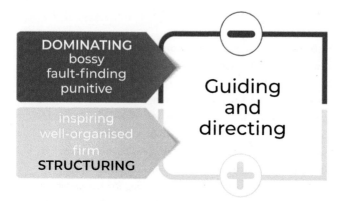

Figure 2.4 Guiding and directing - effective and ineffective behaviours.

The first set of behaviours is collectively referred to as Structuring and the second set as Dominating. Since there are many nuances in between these two sets, any real-life behaviour is more likely to lie on a spectrum between these two sets rather than fitting squarely into one only. A key issue for deciding, however, is how the behaviour is experienced by others, whatever the intention.

With regards to Guiding and Directing others we therefore arrive at the spectrum of possibilities shown in Figure 2.4.

We are talking about "effective" and "ineffective" rather than "good" and "bad" behaviours. This is to acknowledge that real life situations are not polarized as "good" and "bad". Remember that "effective" refers to the degree to which a goal is achieved. So the effectiveness of a behaviour can't be completely divorced from the subtleties of the actual situation.

Generally, however, it is found that on a spectrum ranging from being more Structuring to being more Dominating, a behaviour that represents the Structuring side is more effective in guiding others than behaviours that are Dominating. Dominating behaviours give the message, "You are not good enough". Structuring behaviours give the message, "You can do it, and succeed".

It is important to remember that here we are talking about behaviours and not about personalities. This reflects the freedom of responding rather than the feeling of inevitability of knee-jerk reactions. We are not born and stuck with behaviours. We can learn to choose our behaviour. Once we master choosing our behaviour effectively, i.e. in a way that achieves the goal, we have become fluent at it.

Dominating behaviour is reactive, springing from an emotion such as anger or anxiety, and shows a lack of respect for people. When leaders use Dominating behaviour, people are most likely to respond using another reactive behaviour such as Compliant/Resistant or Immature behaviours.

This then usually leads to an ineffective outcome for the ongoing relationship, and sometimes actual conflict.

Structuring behaviour by a leader is represented by providing people with a kind of scaffold which will enable them to develop and reach their potential. Your own enthusiasm and confidence will inspire people to be motivated, especially if you show confidence in their abilities. It requires you to be well organized in the way you present people with the means to carry out tasks, including clarity of responsibilities, the information needed, or training in the means to acquire information and skills. At the same time, Structuring is about being firm about requirements which cannot be negotiated (such as regulations or conduct, or some other situation where the only option is to tell people what you need them to do). A leader who tells people what they need from them, and why, is being "firm" in the functionally fluent sense.

The key to making the choice to use effective behaviour is Accounting - noticing what is going on; finding out from people; becoming aware of the feelings involved (your own and others) and evaluating the possible consequences.

Case study

Chris is a manager who uses a lot of Dominating behaviour in her management of staff. She tells them how she expects them to do the job without any discussion, and gives feedback which is judgmental about faults which she attributes to people being either "good" or "bad" at the job. She rarely gives praise. Her tone of voice is blaming, for example, "If you had started it earlier, we wouldn't be having to sort out this mess!" and instead of using a problem-solving approach, she sees punishment (a personal put-down) as a way of getting people to "pull their socks up". This may sound rather extreme, but imagine how you would feel on the receiving end of any aspect of this behaviour. What would it do to your motivation?

By contrast, Jay (they/them) has a Structuring approach to guiding and directing staff. They are well-organized in the way they direct the work of their department and in developing the work of individuals. They always ask people for their thoughts on the work and treat their views seriously. Jay ensures they think about the level of experience of each member of the team and work with them so that they feel they have the optimal kind of information and support to do the job well. Jay is clear and firm about rules which cannot be broken and boundaries which cannot be crossed, and explains the reasons for these. Their own hard work and friendly approach is inspiring to the team.

Reflection

Thinking back to the situations you identified in the previous reflection above, consider how, when you were in charge, the effective behaviours played a part in the successful, productive conversation, and how the ineffective behaviours may have influenced the unsatisfactory conversation. What could you have done differently?

As we will see through the other chapters in this book, Structuring behaviour in Guiding and Directing needs to be combined with effective Nurturing behaviour in Looking After People in leadership and management to provide a balance between care and control.

Looking after people – Nurturing or Marshmallowing

Figure 2.5 represents the way we look after people when we are in or have taken charge. It shows the contrasts between the effective and ineffective ways of doing this.

The effective Nurturing behaviours include

* accepting (people as human beings, even if you find them difficult)
* understanding (checking out your understanding of their experience)
* compassionate (showing concern for suffering)

whereas care becomes ineffective once it is overdone towards Marshmallowing

* over-indulgent (giving self or others too much of something)
* inconsistent (saying one thing and doing another)
* smothering (taking over instead of enabling others)

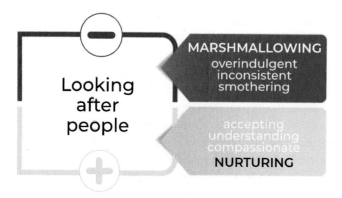

Figure 2.5 Looking after people - effective and ineffective behaviours.

Nurturing behaviour takes account of what is going on for you, the other person, and the situation. It includes appropriate amounts of encouragement and praise. It values and accepts people for who they are, and shows understanding and compassion for individual needs and problems. The message people receive is, "You are valuable". If the Nurturing becomes over-protective, however, it becomes Marshmallowing which is reactive behaviour from emotion such as anxiety about pleasing people. It includes smothering and patronizing others, and stifles growth. Over-indulging can lead to sometimes requiring people to follow rules and standards, and other times not. This is inconsistency which leaves people unsure of where they stand. The behaviour discounts people's own abilities to develop and flourish. The message is, "You are inadequate".

Case study

Ade uses lots of effective behaviours in looking after people in his team. He takes an interest in people as individuals and accepts that people are different and may need different kinds of care and support in order to give their best at work. Parvin is currently having childcare challenges as her husband is very ill and she is having to transport three children to nursery or school before coming to work in the morning.

Ade has shown compassion for Parvin and checked out his understanding of the kinds of support she needs in order to fulfil her role at work, as he does with other parents in a similar position. Together, they have worked out a change to her working hours which suits the whole team.

However, Ade also wastes energy on ineffective Marshmallowing behaviours some of the time. He has become over-protective of a small group in his team whose workload has considerably increased over the last few months. Instead of working out with them what will help them to cope with the increase, he has a tendency to take over substantial amounts of the work himself, making his own workload much heavier, so that he is seldom available to other members of the team. The staff involved have now become resentful that Ade is picking up work which they find more interesting, leaving them with routine work they find less interesting.

With another member of staff, Ade has over-indulged their desire to present to senior managers, preventing other members of the team from having this developmental opportunity.

Reflection

Think about how you do the caring aspect of leadership and management. Do you show caring behaviour but accept that people can also take responsibility for themselves? Or do you sometimes "take over" or indulge people in a way which disempowers them and also means you are taking on more yourself? How could you put more energy into Nurturing instead?

Reflection on the Being-in-Charge behaviours

How much of your time and energy would you estimate is spent with the Golden Five and how much with the Purple Pitfalls of Being in Charge?

As mentioned above, Being-in-Charge behaviours relate to your management of yourself as well as your management of others. If you undermine yourself emotionally or practically by judging yourself harshly, calling yourself names, and blaming yourself for things which are not, or not only, your fault, you are using Dominating behaviours with yourself. If you over-indulge yourself when you are tired or stressed by eating unhealthy foods or drinking too much, or deny yourself in order to please others on a regular basis, you are Marshmallowing yourself.

We can use Structuring and Nurturing behaviours with ourselves to boost our energy and our self-esteem. For example, I am excellent at finding fault with things I have done and telling myself I am an "idiot". However, I am now able to Structure myself by reminding myself that even if I didn't do something as well as I would have liked in that situation, I can learn from the experience, and it doesn't make me an idiot. Sometimes, I will consciously think about how I can Nurture myself better, such as when I told my daughter that I need to wind down after 9 p.m. in the evenings and asking her (who is a night bird) to give me a call earlier.

Relating to others – Cooperative or Compliant/Resistant

Next, we focus on the area of the model shown in Figure 2.6, which represents the way an individual chooses to liaise and cooperate in a relationship when they are in a position of Being an Individual rather than in charge. Our behaviour is always a mixture of styles and these behaviours are still part of your portfolio as a leader or manager. Here the effective Cooperative behaviours include

- friendly (showing genuine warmth)
- assertive (standing up for yourself and negotiating)
- considerate (showing thoughtfulness about others' feelings/point of view)

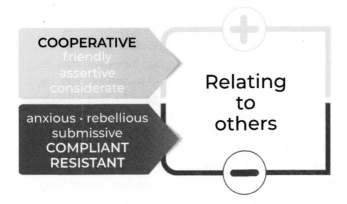

Figure 2.6 Relating to others - ineffective and effective behaviours.

while the Compliant/Resistant ineffective behaviours include

- anxious (showing/feeling worry, nervousness or unease)
- rebellious (resisting authority)
- submissive (conforming to the will of others/assuming they are right)

On first sight it might appear confusing that Compliant and Resistant be-haviours are shown together. This is because being compliant and being resistant have in common that they withdraw active participation in the relationship. In the first case, a person using compliant behaviour says, "I'll do whatever you say and withhold my thoughts on it". In the second case, a person using resistant behaviour says, "Even if I think it is a good idea, I will not do it, just because *you* said it". Both are also reactions to emotion, and are ways we have learnt to relate to others without Accounting for what will work best in the relationship. They may have anxiety or anger/defensiveness as a motivator, or another emotion from a previous experience. Sometimes people flip-flop between Compliant and Resistant behaviour as in the ex-ample of John, below.

True Cooperative behaviour, however, is an active engagement in the relationship, with deliberate responses which show Accounting for the other person's needs, feelings or viewpoints (friendly and considerate) as well as asserting your own needs and views (assertive). Cooperative behaviour is not about giving in to others but negotiating with them on an equal basis, with a focus on reaching a solution which is acceptable to everyone.

Case studies

John is a team leader who sometimes falls into Compliant behaviour and sometimes Resistant behaviour. For him, the Compliant behaviour tends to happen when his Senior Manager, Naomi, attends one of his staff meetings. He finds the experience stressful. Naomi often has an aggressive tone of voice which reminds him of his mother and which makes him feel he has to please her. He often goes away from these occasional meetings feeling he has deferred too much to Naomi, and failed to stand up for himself and his team in discussions. In contrast, when he is presenting to the senior departmental team, he finds it difficult to take criticism of his ideas and finds himself being defensive in his responses. After these meetings, he sometimes wonders why he didn't just discuss the feedback without getting upset.

Julia used to use more Compliant/Resistant behaviour with managers but she has learnt to manage the emotions which used to trigger that behaviour, using breathing and pausing techniques. Now she listens to her Senior Manager's comments with curiosity, asking questions if she feels that assumptions have been made, and providing information which will reassure her manager that she does know what she is doing. She feels that this calmer, Cooperative approach has enabled her manager to trust her, and this has boosted her confidence further. She is not afraid to negotiate respectfully, acknowledging the other's views and concerns and putting forward her arguments. Giving some time to preparation before these encounters has enabled her to explore her awareness of her manager's needs, and assert her own more effectively.

Reflection

Think about when you might fall into the pitfall of Compliant/Resistant behaviour. Do you tend to do one or the other more, or does it depend on the person you are interacting with, or the situation? Which emotions are you feeling when that happens? If you have thought of a specific example, what would you need to take account of to use Cooperative behaviour?

Expressing my own self – Spontaneous or Immature

The fourth element of effective relationships is how you inject your individuality into them as shown in Figure 2.7. Examples of doing this effectively (called Spontaneous) include

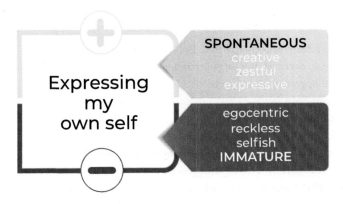

Figure 2.7 Expressing my own self - ineffective and effective behaviours.

- creative (thinking outside the box)
- zestful (sharing personal enthusiasm)
- expressive (conveying thoughts, feelings and ideas)

whereas Immature ineffective ways include

- egocentric (only using own point of view)
- reckless (not heeding danger or consequences of one's actions)
- selfish (concerned only with own needs/pleasure/lacking consideration for others)

The ineffective behaviours here are called Immature because they are behaviours we have not grown out of. They are the ways that a two-year old may express themselves, which is understandable in a small child who doesn't yet have the understanding to take account of the effect of their behaviour on others, or sufficiently complex grasp of language to express themselves fully. As with the other ineffective behaviours, we can all fall into them as a reaction to stress or emotion from time to time.

The effective Spontaneous responses Account for the effect they may have on people around us, which is why we may find them more difficult when we are feeling pressure from the situation or the other people involved. When we are able to "read" the situation and express our inner energy, we will tell people about our needs and views (expressive), show our enthusiasm (zestful) and allow our ideas to flow (creative), thus being more authentically ourselves and bringing our individual character to what we do.

Case study

Grace manages a large team of technical staff. Each day, members of the team are called to different parts of the organization to work on keeping the systems working and upgrading them, or to deal with an emergency. Grace's interactions with them have felt very task- oriented on both sides, although Grace also shows care for staff's needs.

However, staff don't really feel they know Grace as a human being. She is aware she has always been very much "in role" with them. She decides to arrange occasional breakfasts or lunches with groups from the team – a short time when they can chat together about what they did at the weekend, and she can tell them about her own interests and family. The relationship between Grace and her staff retains its professionality but becomes warmer and friendlier, adding to the trust between them.

We have probably all experienced humour being used in very effective ways. At a tense moment in a complex negotiation, for example, an expertly injected humorous comment can lead to the situation being defused, the participants taking a quick break, and returning refreshed. It does take that expert touch though. One can easily imagine how disruptive and ineffective it would be for someone to constantly only inject ridicule and immaturity into a relationship.

The following example demonstrates the expression of self through imagination, curiosity, and innovation.

Case study

During the pandemic, Noah's team began to lose motivation. They were used to collaborating together in the office and enjoyed working with each other. The use of online meetings enabled work to continue, but the meetings didn't have the same energy as before. Noah wondered what he could do about this, and one day as he was out for a walk which helped him to boost his energy, he realized that he could ask the team to do something different for their meetings. There were only four of them and all lived reasonably close to each other in their small town.

Noah suggested they have a walking meeting once a week and each bring along the key issue they wanted to discuss. Some of the members were a bit doubtful that this would enable them to get the work done, and they were behind with their deadlines.

Noah said, "Come on, let's give it a try. I'm curious about how it will work, and I think it will help to boost our discussions by being together (socially distanced of course!) and getting some fresh air as well." Noah's enthusiasm was infectious, and the team agreed. Before long, they realized that the combination of exercise and talking through the issues, when they could gently interrupt each other to build ideas, was enabling them to be more creative too. They decided this should become a regular part of their teamwork, even after they were able to return to work (weather permitting of course!)

Reflection

To what extent do you use Spontaneous behaviour at work/at home? Would your work colleagues be able to describe your individual character, some of your interests, enthusiasms? Are your direct reports able to see the individual, as well as the role? If you think you could be using more Spontaneous behaviour, what holds you back?

A key effect

You may already have realized that a general effect of using Golden Five behaviours or Purple Pitfall behaviours is that they each invite similar behaviours. If a leader or manager is using Dominating or Marshmallowing behaviour, they are likely to receive a reaction from another ineffective behaviour, such as Compliant/Resistant or Immature. If a member of staff is using Compliant/Resistant or Immature behaviour, there is an increased risk that a leader will be drawn into reacting with Dominating or Marshmallowing behaviour. It's easy to see how this can generate a spiral of ineffective behaviours. As the Power of Choice diagram (Figure 2.1) shows, we need to make a choice not to react but to respond.

The good news is that using Golden Five behaviours makes it more likely that you will receive a similar response from others.

Reflection

Consider your experience of a situation in which you used Purple Pitfall behaviour yourself. Did you get a reaction in the form of similar behaviour? Then consider when you have felt drawn into using Purple Pitfall behaviour. Was it triggered by the other person's Purple Pitfall behaviour? What about when you use Golden Five behaviours?

Summary

- Functional Fluency is about the art and skill of effective relationships with others but also with ourselves
- Ineffective behaviours are called the Purple Pitfalls and consist of Dominating, Marshmallowing, Compliant/Resistant, and Immature. They are reactions to emotion, and we all fall into them from time to time
- Effective behaviours are called the Golden Five and consist of Accounting, Structuring, Nurturing, Cooperative, and Spontaneous. They are responses chosen after Accounting (often sub-consciously)
- The key to giving less energy to ineffective behaviours and more to effective behaviours is to use Accounting behaviour
- Using Purple Pitfall behaviours tends to invite others to react with similar ineffective behaviours. Using the Golden Five effective behaviours encourages others to respond with other effective behaviours

The following chapters will help you to explore in more detail how the behaviours described in the Functional Fluency model relate to leadership and management in a variety of situations and roles. You can always return to this chapter to remind yourself about the terms being used. The Golden Five and Purple Pitfall behaviours will always have an initial capital (Structuring, Nurturing, Accounting, Cooperative, Spontaneous, Dominating, Marshmallowing, Compliant/Resistant, Immature) and the sub-elements of those behaviours will be explained as relevant.

Note

1 The Power of Choice © Susannah Temple (2002).

Chapter 3

The Constructive Manager
Creating Effective Relationships

Rona Rowe

Introduction

Being in charge at work is often presented as an expert role, where the job is to know things, get things done based on this knowledge and with all perspectives considered. It is indeed these things, and it is also a learning role. The person in charge rarely knows all the answers. As work and the workplace changes, we need the ability to learn quickly, shift direction, and innovate. We also need greater skills of self-regulation. The ability to develop teams with these capacities becomes central to the role of a successful manager.

You can only do this if you are expected to learn as you go, and if you expect this of yourself. One of the great benefits of using Functional Fluency as a frame of reference to guide your leadership and management journey, is that it assumes that you will develop and should develop. The goal is to grow into a leadership style which allows you to be flexible and balanced in choosing your behaviours so that the energy you use as you interact with your people at work can flow freely and effectively. In this way you can choose a mix of approaches in responding to any situation, thereby giving yourself and your teams the best chance of success.

The Functional Fluency model is described in detail in Chapter 2. In this chapter, I take the perspective of a relatively new manager, or a manager in a new organization, and explain the advantages of the model for the person working in this context.

At the beginning of your management career, one of the most useful ideas to understand and recognize is the difference between responding and reacting. Responding allows you time to do a reality assessment, ensure you have all the information you need, check you've understood 'what's really going on', and then make a choice what to do about it. You can take account of the situation, the task/issue and the people. Reacting is fast, rigid and feels non-negotiable. If you notice yourself saying, '*I had no choice*' a lot, especially in relation to your dealings with other people, it is likely you are reacting not responding.

DOI: 10.4324/9781003345527-3

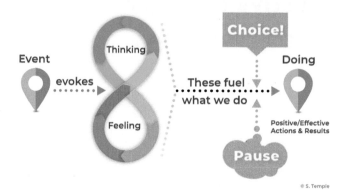

Figure 3.1 ¹The Power of Choice adapted from © SJTemple.

The difference is the functionally fluent pause: a pause taken in awareness and for a purpose. See Figure 3.1.

Your first responsibility is figuring out how you look, sound, feel, and act when you're responsive, and conversely, how you look, sound, feel, and act when you're reactive. A functionally fluent manager understands that how they behave impacts on everyone around them, and sets the cultural tone for the team. Self-awareness and awareness of others is central to constructing yourself as a constructive manager.

Becoming a new manager

So, here you are, promoted or recruited, in charge of your own team or project, faced with a sea of new faces, or well-known faces, now less familiar from your new perspective, all of them looking to you with various degrees of interest, judgement, openness, and resistance. Welcome to management.

Depending on your organization, some things may be clear in this new role – processes, targets, where your team fits in the organization, what you need to get on with, who you are expected to work with, and what you are responsible for. There may be an induction process. You may be excited or nervous, you may feel well supported or not. It's a busy time – and you expected that. There's often an expectation that you hit the ground running. And somewhere is an assumption that an efficient and high performing team will somehow emerge naturally if you simply get on with the work. If you're fortunate, your 'honeymoon' period will last long enough for you to get your feet under the table, find your way around the workplace – either real or virtual – probably both, get a grasp of the basics of your new role before 'something happens', and you are in the middle of your first stress test with your team looking to you to lead them through.

If it wasn't before, it is now clear that your success is dependent on your ability to navigate your working relationship with the people around you – especially your team. Fortunately, Functional Fluency gives you a framework for thinking about what to do. It invites you to step back and take a pause before you act, so you can make effective choices. As you know from Chapter 2, there are five different effective behaviour groups – Structuring, Nurturing, Cooperating, Spontaneous, and Accounting – which you can mix and match as the situation demands. These are the Golden Five.

What you are required to do may be clear, e.g. you've got a last minute order which will require some of your team to work the weekend – but how you approach your team to solve this problem, here you have choice. If you react, your ineffective behaviours invite unhelpful behaviours back. If you respond, choosing to use your energy in more helpful ways, staying with the Golden Five, you invite responsiveness from others. Now, together, you have the capacity to problem solve, fluently, flexibly, and efficiently. When energy is used effectively, decisions can be made with the least amount of distress to everyone.

Under stress, when we are tired and uncertain and resources are stretched, we can all fall into ineffective behaviours. This is when we fall into the Purple Pitfalls. Accounting allows us to move back into the Golden Five to give ourselves the best chance of achieving our goals together. Everyone can feel the difference and see the results. I think of it as 'Going for Gold'.

Over the years, much research has been done, trying to identify what makes a successful organization. Various elements have been identified, but the one that is consistently a key indicator is employee engagement. In Table 3.1[2], the CIPD have indicated the management focuses that underpin employee engagement, and it maps remarkably closely to the model of successful human social functioning that underpins Functional Fluency.

Table 3.1 Summary of 'Managing for sustainable employee engagement framework' from *Managing for sustainable employee engagement: guidance for employers and managers*, CIPD (2012)

Competency	Brief description
Open, fair and consistent	Managing with integrity and consistency, managing emotions/personal issues and taking a positive approach in interpersonal interactions
Handling conflict and problems	Dealing with employee conflicts (including bullying and abuse) and using appropriate organizational resources
Knowledge, clarity and guidance	Clear communication, advice and guidance, demonstrating understanding of roles and responsible decision-making
Building and sustaining relationships	Personal interaction with employees involving empathy and consideration
Supporting development	Supporting and arranging employee career progression and development

Understanding your role

Role theory

Often, this part of your management learning is glossed over in the rush to get on. But it is helpful to become aware that your change in role means changes in all your working relationships, not only from your perspective, but everyone else's too. This is especially true if you have moved from being a team member to a team manager in the same organization.

Role theory is an idea from Organizational Transactional Analysis developed by Bernd Schmid, first published in 2008[3]. According to this theory we inhabit 3 worlds: private, professional, and organizational. Within each of these worlds we have many roles, represented by the subdivisions. A role is a coherent pattern of feelings, thoughts, behaviours, perspectives on reality, and relationships (Figures 3.2 and 3.3).

Figure 3.2 The Three Worlds we inhabit.

Figure 3.3 The Three Worlds with role divisions.

So, in your private world, for example, you may be a partner, a parent, a son or daughter. Your role as a parent may require you to be a taxi driver, homework supporter, chef, cleaner, etc. You may also be a climate activist and a local councillor too. In your professional world you may be an accountant, a colleague, an expert witness, a member of a professional body. Your organizational role includes your role as an employee. You may also be a manager, a budget holder, a partnership worker, a committee member.

The usefulness of this model is that it explains the discomfort which accompanies the change from team member to manager – and the many other role changes you may encounter. A new manager now has many more organizational roles which take up much more of their time and focus, and these require a shift in their relationships and their perspectives on reality. No wonder the transition is sometimes unexpectedly challenging – everything shifts: each of our new roles will stimulate different feelings, thoughts, and behaviours in us. Until we become a manager, we have often had to account mostly for our professional self. Now we have an organizational self to account for, and all our different roles in that world.

Here are three ways of thinking about different challenges we can face in our roles and worlds.

Role confusion

In role confusion, illustrated in Figure 3.4, one or more of your roles, *within one world*, come into conflict. For example in your role as member of the leadership team you may have to cut your payroll costs by 10% in the next financial year. This information is not to be made public for the next few months, but planning must start now. As manager of your high performing team, this feels unfair and yet these are the expectations and decisions required of you.

Figure 3.4 Role confusion.

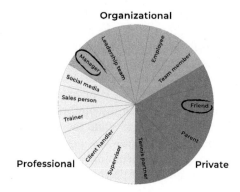

Figure 3.5 Role contamination.

Role contamination

In role contamination, shown in Figure 3.5, there is potential conflict between roles *in different worlds*. Here the private world has contaminated the
organizational world. You may now be managing your friend. Both of these
relationships will need some renegotiation to take account of the circumstances. In the old days, you may have told your friend everything, now it
may not be appropriate. Also if you are too 'friendly' at work, how will this
affect the other team members – a danger perhaps of accusations of fa-
vouritism even with no evidence. But these are now the rocky paths for a
new manager to navigate.

Role exclusion

Finally there is exclusion, as shown in Figure 3.6 – the absence of a whole
world. Here it's shown as the exclusion of the professional world. This might

Figure 3.6 Role exclusion – professional world.

Figure 3.7 Role exclusion – private world.

be a newly promoted manager who gets swept off her feet into the corridors of power and distant board rooms. Engulfed in her organizational roles, she neglects to give time to sharing her professional expertise with the team to inform them and support their problem-solving.

In a different scenario, shown in Figure 3.7, you can see how sometimes private worlds can suffer when individuals are promoted and more is expected of them at work – not just their regular hours, but out-of-hours entertaining of clients and working weekends. This is a useful model to check the balance in your life, and ensure you are paying attention to your roles in *all* your worlds. It's another way of looking at work-life balance.

Accounting for the roles you are in at any time will help you to use the Golden Five behaviours most effectively.

Reflection

Draw your own role diagram. Where and with whom are you most likely to come into potential 'conflict'? Is there any shift in behaviour which might help you navigate this relationship more effectively?

'Rookie' mistakes

When you first become a manager, you take into the role your previous experiences of other managers you have had in your career, and often the style of 'managing' you encountered in the family that raised you. Whether you are aware of it or not, you have made certain decisions about what a manager does and doesn't do, how they behave, how they use the power of their position, and what they expect from their colleagues – subordinate, peer or superior.

Most of these decisions have been made in other contexts, at other times and in other circumstances. Many of them will be informing how you behave when you become the manager. How useful they are to you in your current circumstances will depend on your capacity to examine your behaviours, understand them as chosen, not fixed, and adapt them to your here-and-now reality.

Here are some commonly held 'assumptions' which can hold you back.

Managers must always show they are in charge

In Functional Fluency terms this means you spend all your time Guiding and Directing and Looking after People, and don't think to spend time Relating to Others and Expressing Your Own Self.

Case study

I knew a manager like this once. 'If only people would just do as I say, we'd be fine,' she would lament regularly. This was just one manifestation of her Dominating judgemental, 'I know better' behaviours which kept the team locked in to doing their own thing their own way (if they could get away with it), or obeying the letter of her instructions, no more no less, and as a result feeling dissatisfied and disempowered. As things went wrong, this manager did more and more of the same: more instruction, more blaming the team, more Dominating behaviours. She herself might have described her choices as being 'firm and consistent' but she was not getting the results she wanted. Her frustration with the resistance she provoked took a lot of energy away from the tasks at hand. This manager, in many circumstances, exhibited effective Structuring behaviours – well-organized, clear reporting and writing, worked well with people who had strengths like her own, and would fight for her team in the wider organization. And yet it was exhausting working for a manager who was so often disappointed.

The energy shift came when a new team member 'found' the manager's sense of humour, and her hitherto hidden infectious laughter rang out occasionally across the office. This new team member also exhibited many Nurturing behaviours to all the team members, including the manager. The increase in Nurturing and Spontaneous behaviours allowed the energy in the team to open up. People relaxed, the manager was able to listen to feedback, to collaborate more on decision-making, and team members felt more inclined to share ideas. Everyone benefited.

The manager's lament continued, but the fault-finding quality that had felt so crushing was now understood as an expression of managerial 'foot-stamping' meant to let off steam not to undermine the morale of the team. This manager gradually added to her repertoire of functionally fluent behaviours and, as her capacity to be flexible developed, the team came to appreciate her already well-honed Directing and Guiding skills. It is important to remember in this model that Structuring and Nurturing are connected – you can't exhibit one without the other. So Structuring without Nurturing becomes Dominating, and Nurturing without Structuring becomes Marshmallowing.

Simply telling your team what to do doesn't guarantee success. It *is* your role as manager to know what needs to be done. And that can be achieved in many different ways. There are managers and organizations where staff intimidation and bullying are the dominant culture, but this only 'works' when there are lots of resources available so people are easily expendable, and high staff turnover doesn't matter to the quality of the output. In the long term it doesn't work. It is inefficient, unpleasant, and the price in terms of human wellbeing, as well as the economic cost, is high.

Another unintended consequence of this managerial assumption, is the development of a dependent culture, where staff stop thinking for themselves and wait to be told what to do. Proactive and problem-solving individuals are a prerequisite for a productive team, but this strongly directive leadership can encourage passivity, creating even more work for the manager. It doesn't take long for resentments to bubble up and Compliant/Resistant behaviours to dominate the culture.

Reflection

Do you know the difference between your Structuring and Dominating behaviours? Describe them to a trusted colleague. Do they agree?

Managers must always look after their teams: needing to be needed

There is often a misunderstanding about what it means to be a caring manager. We can think that we have to save our team from every discomfort or challenge that comes their way. This is not the role of a manager. Each person is responsible for their own well-being. This is made easier if you have a manager who is accepting and understanding and cheers you on, values you and your work, and finds ways to let you know these things. You need a secure base at work that allows you to perform and develop in your role and take responsibility for yourself.

Caring behaviours which are ineffective are over-indulgent, over-tolerant, over-protective, and inconsistent. Managers can end up doing their team's jobs for them, working long hours to 'rescue' the team from somebody else's incompetence. These managers can be heard saying, '*I might as well do it myself,*' instead of handing back work which needs to be redone in order to avoid the challenging conversation that needs to be had. These managers often feel responsible for their team members' feelings, so they avoid being direct about expectations and boundaries. This creates confusion instead of a secure-enough base to get on with the job, where each individual is confident in their role, and the outcome expected of them.

Nurturing behaviours empower staff to want to do well, to seek help when required so they can succeed, not to encourage dependency and being able to 'get out of' doing what is required. Marshmallowing behaviours ultimately disempower your staff even though you may have intended to be 'helpful' and caring. This can be a difficult balance to find as a new manager but it is crucial to pay attention to it.

As soon as you can see yourself putting your own wellbeing at the bottom of the pile – working late for your team members, coming into work tired and grumpy, being unexpectedly short-tempered with your staff – these are all signs that you may have got out of balance and need to do some Accounting – evaluating, asking yourself a few questions about how effectively you are caring for your team and yourself.

One of the most useful aspects of this model is understanding that, as adults, we are all responsible for Structuring and Nurturing ourselves whatever our roles. When you are responsible for others, it can take some self-discipline to incorporate this idea into your own functionally fluent leadership.

Good managers are well-liked: wanting to be liked

Often new managers get out of kilter because they want to be liked. It's hard to figure out how to stay connected with staff, and to hold the appropriate boundaries now your role has changed. Resisting the temptation to make decisions on the basis of being liked, and focusing on how to get the job done well using the resources for the benefit of all, is far more sustainable, and will earn you respect in the long run. None of this is necessarily easy but it is possible, if you develop your functionally fluent behaviours, notice when Nurturing turns into Marshmallowing for you, and put in place strategies to keep your energy working from the Golden Five.

Being a manager requires you to be aware of the boundaries between you and other members of staff. Boundaries are the way we keep our roles and responsibilities clear and enable us to be effective.

Case study

James had been promoted internally, and he was about to have an appraisal meeting with his team member who was also his long-time gym buddy. As friends, they knew a lot about each other, and there remained a temptation to ignore the new roles and just 'have a chat' in their usual fashion. But James knew that it was his responsibility to support Mike's work and challenge him to develop and perform well. It was no longer appropriate to disclose everything he was thinking; he now had access to organizational knowledge which was sensitive and confidential. How easy it would be to favour Mike over other team members.

Whilst at work, it was James' job to be Mike's manager first and friend second – and if those came into conflict, his responsibility was first to the organization. James chose to have an upfront conversation with Mike about this and his worries about 'getting it right'. They understood that their conversations at the gym would not include work gossip in the way they once had. They agreed to work through the discomfort, be honest about their feelings, and check in if the boundaries appeared to be getting blurred. They Accounted for the change, and Cooperated in a plan of how to move forward. The relationship prospered, both professionally and personally. Both of them agreed that this probably would not have been the case if they had not had this conversation up-front.

And this strategy may not have worked for everyone. James has a responsibility to think about the wider team. Are others looking on in resentment, is distrust growing, is Mike seen as 'favoured' because of his relationship with James? This situation can have a de-stabilizing effect on the team, even if James and Mike are able to navigate it easily. In this case, James may have to take the decision to stop visiting the gym with Mike. Navigating this situation will require all James's capacities to use the Golden Five behaviours effectively.

Reflection

What ideas/assumptions about your leadership and management do you hold to be true? How functionally fluent do these assumptions allow you to be?

Managing performance

Giving feedback is a key function of a manager – it allows you to set expectations, and direction. Done well, it lowers resistance, means less time is wasted, and the team is kept focused – which maximizes the chance of success and responsiveness to change when circumstances require. It builds trust and resilience.

A manager who can offer a difficult message to an individual or a team, in a functionally fluent way, will have the best chance of being heard, and the message being taken on board, because there will have been an Accounting for the needs of the people, the situation, and the shared purpose.

Another important aspect of managing performance is noticing what people are doing right and giving them credit for their successes. What you choose to celebrate with your team sets the tone. Under pressure, this positive feedback can get lost in the need to problem-solve and get things 'right'. The problem of giving in to this approach is that the ratio of negative feedback to positive feedback becomes unhelpful and individual performance may dip[4]. A key characteristic of high performing individuals and teams is that they demonstrate much more positive feedback than negative which sustains and motivates high performance[5].

Functional Fluency shares many of the values of Positive Psychology, being essentially a strength-based system, inviting you to notice your effective behaviours – in other words, what you do that works - and expand your use of these behaviours to develop effective and healthy working relationships. A system where positive feedback is scarce does not sustain a high performing team. The positive feedback also needs to be well-targeted, timely, and evidence-based. It is equally as important in clarifying goals and expectations as the redirecting function of 'negative' feedback. Psychologically, a team where smiles and appreciation are valued, that expects to give and receive approbation and encouragement for a job well done, is more likely to perform well, be resilient when times get tough, and sustain itself over time. You do not have to be a smiley boss to run a functionally fluent team. This does not stop you appreciating smiles in others, and you may regularly send appreciative emails when colleagues do something outstanding, or small things that make a difference. These are also positive feedback behaviours.

When things go wrong, very few functionally fluent managers spend their energy finding out who is to blame. More likely they will be using their energies to find out what happened and why, for the purpose of framing the learning opportunity. This will include holding people to account, so mistakes can be put right and improvements can be made. When the purpose of challenge is clear and expressed, it is easier for everyone to own their mistakes, be accountable for their actions, and try again.

Case study

As discussed earlier in this chapter, managers often have pre-conceptions that Dominating behaviours are required for them to be effective. Mahmoud said that 'being judgemental' and finding who was 'at fault' was part of his role. We talked about how effective he thought his feedback was for his team. Did they change their behaviours, did performance improve? He described how tired he got telling them again and again what they were doing wrong. What he noticed was that his feedback worked in the short-term but it had no staying power. Also (I noticed) he had no time for positive feedback because he had to spend so much time keeping 'on top of' the 'shirkers'. When I asked him to Account for the lack of effectiveness of his feedback, he said he had no idea, and then made some general disparaging comment about the quality of the staff.

He himself presented as a straight talking, no-nonsense kind of person, very neat in appearance, someone with high standards. He wanted to improve the performance of his team. We talked about doing some Accounting first – analyzing where his team members were failing. Were there individuals whose behaviour needed to be addressed? Were there patterns to be noticed, e.g. the morning shift performed worse than the afternoon – and why was that? In the course of our conversations, I could see Mahmoud getting curious, open to possibility. Instead of starting with judgment, Mahmoud started with purpose – performance improvement – and then he got curious. As often happens, our Spontaneous behaviours invite Co-operation with others. He explained his purpose to his team and asked for input from his staff – why did they think standards were slipping? What he discovered was a whole mix of issues which he could address, and some that needed to be escalated upwards.

As his enquiries continued, a number of his team members offered ideas to change shift patterns which the whole team welcomed. For the team members who had to improve their own performances, informal training sessions with more experienced members of staff proved popular. Mahmoud simply had to give his permission for this to be a legitimate use of time (Structuring). And inevitably there were the few who needed him to be firm, pointing out the gap between expectations and performance, and using the company structures available to terminate their contracts when required. This was now a rare occurrence, creating much less agitation in the team and himself. He was, he admitted, using much less energy and the performance of his team was improving. Others had noticed too.

Mahmoud's understanding of this work was that his willingness to reframe his purpose, from making judgments to improving performance, had encouraged him to be curious about how to do this (Spontaneous), encouraged him to enquire (Accounting) about the performance levels and the knowledge in the team members that might be useful. Unexpectedly, this had given him a lot of useful knowledge, and uncovered a willingness to co-operate for mutual benefit by many of the team members, which he could then facilitate (Co-operative). He had discovered for himself that helpful Structuring was so much more effective than judgemental Dominating when it came to creating a high performing team.

Every feedback situation is unique because each individual is unique and with a functionally fluent approach you can respond in the here-and-now even when circumstances aren't ideal.

Case study

Martha had years of experience in her profession, and was now a new manager. She was excited, ready for a new challenge – and she got one. Her team had a very new member of staff who had been put into the organization's poor performance process almost as soon as he'd been through his induction period. She was now the manager who needed to work through the capability process with him. She did it, and he successfully got back on track. Six months later, he gave her a glowing endorsement as a manager as part of a 360 feedback process. Martha was delighted – and a little amazed! What had she done to achieve this?

This is how she described it. I paraphrase.

First, she had a moment of panic, took a deep breath, and thought, 'Here we go, baptism by fire'. Then she did some reality testing: what did she have, going into this process? She had her confidence in her knowledge of the staff-member's role – she'd done it for many years before becoming a manager. The organization's capability process was clear too. On the other hand, she didn't know the staff member at all. So, in their first meeting, she asked what he needed from her to give himself the best chance of success and that would allow the difficult process to be as ok as possible. He said, 'You've got to be straight with me, I can't bear fussing, I get lost and then I don't know what to do.' Martha was quite happy to do this as it suited her working style anyway – 'a bit of luck'. Because it had been agreed, and her first thought had been for the needs of the member of staff (Nurturing), Martha's direct approach was experienced as Co-operative and Structuring rather than Dominating and the usual levels of anxiety round the process were much reduced. Her member of staff could respond to her feedback, do what was required without high levels of defensiveness, and succeed. He was obviously delighted and chose to voluntarily use his own professional capability experience to explain her qualities as a manager as part of an entirely separate staff feedback opportunity! Something so daunting for all parties was transformed into an experience of mutual benefit.

Martha's own reflection was that she also uses humour at work to lighten the sometimes very stressful and high risk business she is in – for herself and her colleagues. In this particular example, she felt that, in some of the more difficult feedback conversations they had, her capacity to lighten the mood was helpful for them both. So in Functional Fluency terms, there was an Accounting for her strengths and resources, enquiring about needs (Nurturing) which framed their process as Co-operative. A judicious use of her own Spontaneous playful energy provided some useful oiling of the wheels which contributed to the building of a strong working alliance in the most challenging of circumstances. In my view, it helped that Martha trusted the organization's process to hold the Structuring needed to facilitate a successful outcome.

This is an example of the flexibility of Functional Fluency, mixing all of the different effective behaviours in response to the specific needs of a situation. The model is an invitation to do differently, to notice your choices, and Account for your strengths.

One of the great gifts a manager can give a team is the experience of effective feedback both challenging and encouraging, and opportunities to learn how to give effective feedback themselves.

Learning and development

Developing staff

As managers, we understand our main responsibility is to ensure our team 'gets the job done' on time, in budget, and with the least amount of deviation and disruption to the process as possible. Along the way we pay attention to the wellbeing and resilience of our staff as we look to sustain and improve their performance. For this we need a resourced and engaged workforce – and that doesn't just happen. Even if you can offer your staff a good salary and a comprehensive benefit package, it might not be enough. Up to a point humans are motivated by money and status (and some of us more than others), but eventually we are motivated by other, more nuanced drivers, like purpose and connection, and personal and professional growth. A powerful contributor to staff engagement has been shown to be a commitment to staff development by the organization. When our development needs are accounted for, we feel connected, stimulated, and valued. The Structuring, Nurturing, and Cooperative behaviours which commitment to staff development entails, are powerful motivators.

And it is not only the individuals in your team who need developing; so does the organization. The present is only today, the future is close by – full of possibility, challenge and change. Who could have known in 2019, for example, that we would all need to facilitate some of our key workplace relationships online, and in the process be able to navigate video conferencing software, wireless networks, and bandwidth issues? What must that have been like for a team whose manager had not encouraged online literacy of her staff before the Covid-19 pandemic hit us; how much bigger a disruption to 'getting the job done' and more difficult a process to be part of and to manage?

However unpredictable the future, it is your role as a manager to consider what is coming over the horizon in your business, and make plans to prepare your staff for this. This preparation is bound to include some learning and development. Ensuring that your team is future-ready gives you and them a huge advantage. It connects the organization's future to the individuals' – it aligns the content of your work with a wider strategy, and when purposes are aligned throughout an organization, it lowers anxiety, promotes solution-focussed collaborative working, and encourages greater autonomy in decision-making. There is confidence in coherence – people know the part they play in the wider picture, and can settle into their roles. They experience a systemic Accounting for different points of view.

Taking a meta-level perspective, learning itself requires flexibility, risk taking, and a willingness to change; at the very least to integrate new ideas into current frames of reference. This in itself makes individuals more agile when faced with changing circumstances. In Accounting for differing learning needs and styles, and ensuring that Spontaneous energy imbues the experience, development is kept relevant and enjoyable. A balancing of Structuring and Nurturing focuses on people and outcome, whilst Cooperative behaviours from design to delivery ensure the development is best suited to the learners it is designed to support. Functional Fluency is a model based on the idea that things are always changing, and each of us has the capacity to respond flexibly and in a balanced way to the benefit of all.

Developing yourself

Developing yourself matters too. If we keep learning, our brains stay flexible and we can respond to unexpected changes with curiosity and an expectation of a successful transition. A different future seems possible, even when it has been forced on you. This capacity to stay positive, and hold the hope of a brighter future when things are tough, is a highly valuable quality in a manager. As you develop your own management style, you need some investment in your own growth, and support and encouragement to learn. Your capacity to Nurture yourself, and Structure your time and space for your own development aspirations and goals, sets a functionally fluent example for your team.

Case study

I had a conversation with a successful manager who had taken on a failing team and turned them around to a high performing, self-supporting group of professionals, who could respond to changes at a micro and macro level, without undue agitation or wasted energy. They self-reported high levels of satisfaction; staff absenteeism, and client complaints were low. They wanted to come to work in spite of the high risk, high stress environment that met them each day; they were committed to their clients and their colleagues.

In spite of all this success, the manager was thinking of leaving. What, I wondered, was the difference in her circumstances compared to that of her team? Her conclusion was that the successful transformation of that team had been based on her commitment to their development – individually and as a group. What was different in her case? No one, currently, was encouraging or supporting her own development – she didn't even have a personal development plan. (There hadn't been time!). She didn't feel connected or particularly valued except by her team. In fact, she felt 'used' and 'taken for granted'.

Although we would have more work to do to prove a direct causal link in this instance, given the strength of evidence in other research on staff engagement, it would be a reasonable hypothesis that some learning and development might make a difference to this manager's current attitude to her work. This organization risked losing a valuable member of staff with a proven track record of handling one of the most difficult challenges facing a new manager – sorting out a failing team.

Becoming a functionally fluent manager is a learning process in itself. It encourages you to challenge yourself continually, putting learning and development, your own and others', at the heart of your management practice.

Reflection

Consider your own experience of being managed by others. Have you noticed different attitudes to learning and development in your own bosses?

What impact have those attitudes had on your own engagement and motivation at different moments in your career?

The power of Accounting

Uncertainty

Uncertainty means stress for every human being, at work or not. Uncertainty is qualitatively different to 'change' which can be more easily managed, in the sense that often the change has an outcome or a goal, and therefore a direction. Or, something has happened which has caused change which needs some response. Individuals and groups may be more or less open to a change process, depending on how resilient they are to begin with and how much they perceive the change as negatively or positively impacting on them.

But with uncertainty, everyone is stressed, sympathetic nervous systems are triggered, our fight and flight systems stand guard, ready to protect us from threat. Or we freeze, which in this situation often manifests itself as denial and a refusal to engage with what is actually happening. It is quite possible for what has been a generally positive work team to regress into an anxious and wary group of people, hypervigilant to threat and over-reactive to the most benign of enquiries, or glassy-eyed and passive, hoping it will all go away. And most of this is happening very fast and outside of conscious awareness. Your response as a manager can add fuel to the flames, or help your colleagues settle into a more productive frame of mind. Functional Fluency invites you to notice.

Accounting behaviours allow you to slow down: to self-regulate, so you can use your rational mind to figure out how to shift from less to more helpful behaviours, both in relation to yourself and others. This slowing down is not the same as being slow to respond. It relates to which parts of the brain are available to you in decision making. You need your brain's executive functions to be 'online' to recognize that you have choices. This means you are able to respond in awareness, rather than be at the mercy of your instinctive reactions designed to protect you from physical threat. Ancient mechanisms drive these lightning-quick reactions. Your higher cognitive functions are slower – by milliseconds. These milliseconds matter. Accounting allows enough time for you to recognize that the unfair and critical email from your boss is not the same as a sabre-tooth tiger on the attack. You *can* counteract your ancient brain's initial reaction.

Accounting is reality testing. We are all more likely to fall into Purple Pitfalls when we face uncertainty, because uncertainty by its nature makes us feel unsafe. Accounting allows us to see what is going on and reset the course. The transition from Dominating behaviours, for example, to Structuring behaviours requires the filter of Accounting. It is the mechanism by which we notice that our behaviours are not working, and decide to change.

The wider perspective – what else is going on?

Accounting also includes awareness of the environment 'out there' and as a manager, although you may be managing your team and its day-to-day functioning, you might also think about taking a broader perspective. There are often things happening at an organizational or departmental level which may impact your team and their work.

As a manager, you can make fundamental attribution errors, thinking, for example, that work is not getting done because your team aren't doing their jobs as they should. Whereas organizational and departmental influences may also be at play. Take the example of a university admissions office. Every summer, the admissions team are overwhelmed by their workload – the vast majority of student admissions needing to be processed in a short period of time, ready for the new academic year. This is not the team's issue but the organization's. Without an increase in capacity, the team is always going to struggle at this time of year. The manager needs to acknowledge the reality, and focus on structuring the process, supporting and resourcing the staff and protecting them from the inevitable complaints of anxious and frustrated students and their families.

The structure of an organization itself can create its own challenges. For example, many organizations now use matrix management systems where working relationships, including management relationships, take place across functional and business groups. Staff may report to a line manager and one or more project managers, and some or all of these may be remotely located. This gives an additional challenge to working relationships. The advantages of the system can only be achieved "by building the skills and mindset necessary to cut through the complexity[6]. At the top of these skills is collaboration as members of the matrix often need to work out their own solutions to conflicting priorities, rather than referring this upwards. Indeed, they are likely to be the best able to understand the conflict. The collaboration requires them to be able to take account of the whole picture and the needs of their colleagues (Accounting), and negotiate a solution, being assertive, friendly and helpful, and using creative and imaginative thinking (Cooperative and Spontaneous). Clearly, using functionally fluent behaviours is a key skill for those in a matrix system to develop.

Accounting invites you to consider whatever perspectives might be useful to inform your work and lead your team. It is never too early to look around and see where it might be useful to network. Knowing what's going on in procurement, for example, may have implications for marketing. Production priorities may change because of strategic decisions being made elsewhere.

Politics may be relevant too. Of course, you are not expected to know everything about everything, or even something about everything, but a healthy curiosity and awareness of the wider context in which you are managing your team may pay dividends in the future. Certainly as you move up through the hierarchy of the organization or move on in your career, your capacity for making sense of different perspectives, and developing and using networks, becomes an ever more valuable part of your skillset as a leader and manager.

The enquiring manager

Another aspect of Accounting that I've learnt to pay attention to is Enquiry; in other words asking questions to check your understanding of here-and-now reality.

Case study

The value of this became evident when I worked with a manager and his team a few years ago. David had a big engineering project to design and deliver over 18 months or so – it was the first project he was solely responsible for, so a lot was at stake. David presented as a careful, thoughtful manager who had put a lot of effort into planning this project, taking into account different perspectives, checking assumptions, using the team's knowledge and skills to create the best pathway to success. His bosses were happy with the plan, the team was excited, all was ready, and David launched his plan full of optimism and confidence.

A couple of months passed and the next time we met, David was rather quiet. He was feeling frustrated and dejected. The "wonder" project was not going to plan: the team, he felt, were responsible - not meeting the milestones, seeming unmotivated, and not responding to any encouragement; though by now 'encouragement' (at least to my ears) sounded more like a series of terse emails demanding answers to why things were going wrong, rather than anything remotely Nurturing.

Together we agreed to do some Accounting, looking at the project in the here-and-now. We went through six aspects of Accounting. What did he need to be alert to? A looming critical deadline. What was he aware of? The project not working. How did he know? The project was behind schedule and the Board was getting nervous. Reputations were at stake (evaluation).

How grounded was he when reviewing this project? 'Not very', was the answer. The slide from high hopes to disappointment had been so rapid, that

David was mostly wrapped up in his feelings and who was to blame. Once that reality was named, David could put his feelings to one side and let his rational mind check out what was really going on with this project. A number of things had changed in the context of the team – a key member had left and been replaced. A number of things had changed in the context of the project – a usually reliable supplier had some production problems. The plan needed to be adjusted, some contracts needed to be renegotiated, and the team needed some direction. So David went back to the team, and together they figured out what they needed to get back on track.

In using the process of Accounting we slowed down the thinking process, took a pause to recognize the manager's own feelings, and what really emerged was that David had stopped enquiring about the project in any meaningful way once the planning was done. The team had been left to 'get on with it.' David was not Accounting for the importance of the project to the company both financially and reputationally, and therefore the scrutiny the team felt under to 'get everything right'. Also he had not really accounted for the impact of the key member of staff leaving – years of experience in the field, contacts on the ground that were no longer available to the team, left a big hole in the team's confidence and resources.

David thought he had done his enquiring up-front in the planning stage – and he had. But as this experience showed, change happens all the time, and its impact needs to be accounted for, again and again. A great plan, without a leader with an enquiring mindset, is vulnerable. David set himself the goal of asking more leadership questions, and sustaining this focus over the long term.

Relating Functional Fluency to other management theories

Practising Functional Fluency in management and leadership doesn't require you to set aside other concepts and theories you may have learnt about. Throughout this book we show you how it can enhance your use of other well-regarded models relevant to the theme of the chapter. In this chapter, I've chosen to do this with the Blake Mouton managerial grid, and Daniel Goleman's five domains of emotional intelligence.

The Blake Mouton managerial grid

Functional Fluency is particularly concerned with human social functioning, so its focus is on the relationships you create, and how you use your energy

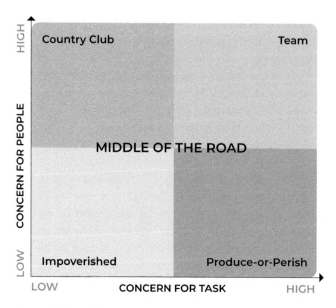

Figure 3.8 Blake Mouton Managerial Grid.

to facilitate these alliances. Although we might assert that your performance at work and that of your team is primarily dependent on your ability to do this effectively, you are also being paid for something else i.e. your economic purpose. To make sense, Functional Fluency is most usefully applied to a defined context and purpose. There will be tasks required, goals to achieve, and targets to meet.

The Blake Mouton Managerial Grid[7] (see Figure 3.8) provides a useful tool for balancing your thinking and prompting you to consider where you direct your attention. The grid has 2 axes:

- X = Concern for Production (Task/Results)
- Y = Concern for People

Looking at this grid through a Functional Fluency lens might be useful in two different ways.

Firstly, if you know you are a people person, you need to take account of your role in supporting your staff to achieve their goals, which may require more focus on task. In Functional Fluency terms, this means effective Guiding and Directing, using Structuring behaviours. And vice versa, if you identify yourself as focusing on task-centred working, then the grid suggests you should shift your focus on to your people and engage with them and what they may need from you, using effective Nurturing behaviours.

There are five styles of leadership behaviour associated with different parts of the grid.

Team style – high people/high task

Blake and Mouton suggest that the Team Style associated with high focus on both people and task (top right quadrant) is the best style in an ideal world. Here a leader motivates their team to work together to succeed. They communicate clearly expectations and task goals. They approach their leadership through the prism of accountability and empowerment, and they are well-organized. There is also an expectation of high levels of team engagement. All the positive behavioural modes of Functional Fluency will be on display when managing in this effective quadrant – a high concern for both people and task requiring a complex juggling of responses, moment to moment, as the situation changes and new needs arise. Especially when conditions are not quite so 'ideal', the reality checking that happens when we are exercising our Accounting muscles encourages a more fluid response to what needs to be dealt with. A functionally fluent leader is not so concerned with their own 'style', but with what works and what doesn't. Their focus is on their capacity to expand their effective behaviours and minimize their ineffective ones.

Country club style – high people/low task

The atmosphere is often friendly but the boundaries are sometimes blurred, and the task lacks priority so performance becomes a problem. This is often the comfort zone of leaders who like to be liked. The manager may be using appropriate Nurturing behaviours but with a lack of Structuring (helping the team to perform through setting boundaries, being helpful and inspiring people to achieve), the task doesn't get done. The effect is then of Marshmallowing.

Impoverished style – low people/low task

Here is the disengaged leader or the paralyzed leader who is afraid of making mistakes. Not surprisingly, this is the least effective approach to leadership. There is a lack of Golden Five behaviours.

Middle-of-the-road style – mid people/mid task

This is an unsatisfactory leadership style. There is not enough concern for the task or the people. There is low energy and low conviction at the top which soon seeps into the team. Nothing matters very much. Initially this can feel quite liberating as people can 'get away' with doing things their own way. A team can limp along like this for a while, but eventually apathy will begin to emerge, and a general malaise show. In the end, people leave; in the end, no one likes to 'not matter'. This style is likely to be characterized by a lack of Accounting, as well as other functionally fluent behaviours. The leader may be inconsistent.

Produce-or-perish style – low people/high task

Leaders control and dominate and expect obedience. Motivation is fed by fear. This leadership style spends most of its energy using Dominating behaviours, and is based on assumptions about how people are, and therefore how they 'have' to be led.

Reflection

Analyze your work week – what percentage of your time is task-focused and how much is people-focused? Have you got the balance right? How do you know? What might you do differently in order to be more effective?

Mark your place on the grid in terms of what you do right now. You may shift positions in different circumstances, depending on the tasks or the people involved. If this is the case, mark more than one position. Now use the Functional Fluency model to move you towards your more desired position. What do you need to do more of or less of? Note these as actions or expectations of yourself. Return to your grid in a month and see if anything has changed.

Daniel Goleman's emotionally intelligent leadership

Functional Fluency is closely connected with the ideas of emotional intelligence, a phrase originally coined by Peter Salovey[8] and popularized by Daniel Goleman and colleagues[9]. In the preface of his 2020 book, *The New Leaders*[10], Goleman et al. write:

> *'The fundamental task of leaders ... is to prime good feeling in those they lead. That occurs when a leader creates resonance – a reservoir of positivity that frees the best in people. At its root the primal job of leadership is emotional.'*

This, they say, determines effectiveness. A leader's (and therefore manager's) emotions have an enormous impact on those they lead for better or for worse. So the need for self-awareness on these matters is key. In the same way, Functional Fluency assumes a high degree of self-awareness to be able to respond in the here-and-now, shifting energy through the behaviour modes to respond to the needs of the situation at hand, and particularly noticing when

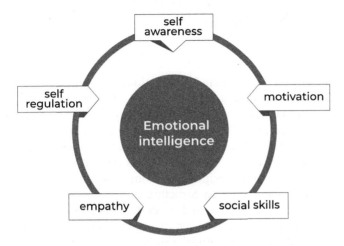

Figure 3.9 Five domains of emotional intelligence.

emotions get hooked and people have moved into more reactive Purple Pitfall behaviours, away from the Golden Five behavioural zones. This kind of awareness requires a high degree of emotional intelligence.

Goleman defines five domains of emotional intelligence as shown in Figure 3.9.

1   Awareness of emotions in self
2   Regulation of emotions in self
3   Motivation – hopeful, clear, purposeful, energetic
4   Awareness of emotions in others – capacity for empathy
5   Regulation of emotion in others – the ability to manage the feelings of others in relationship without becoming dysregulated yourself.

The emotionally intelligent manager doesn't flare up unexpectedly, doesn't take criticism personally, listens to different viewpoints with equanimity, is available to relax and enjoy the people around them appropriately and authentically. This manager is calm in a crisis, makes fair and informed decisions, is inspiring and easy to talk to.

This paragon of emotional virtue may be a vision to aspire to, but for most of us can seem out of reach. The joy of Functional Fluency is that the model includes and expects our natural imperfect selves to turn up every day, and gives us a framework for noticing the different kinds of ineffective behaviours, often driven by our emotional dysregulation, in small and large ways. Through Accounting, we can embrace the pause which allows us to think again, and turn our rational mind to what's up with me, you, them, or the situation - and return to an emotionally regulated space which allows us to get on together for our shared purpose.

Reflection

How comfortable are you with different kinds of emotion, a) in yourself and b) in others? Give yourself a score on a scale of 1 to 10. Where might you concentrate your efforts to increase your emotional intelligence?

Live and let live is not a useful modus operandi when you have a culture and team to lead. You construct your team for better or for worse. Functional Fluency encourages you to be aware of this process and your part in it. It provides a roadmap and a recipe for working well with others in all your roles. It invites you not only to Structure and Nurture the relationships in the team, but to encourage and be part of some robust assertiveness and friendly co-operating to keep the team motivated and engaged with their tasks and goals. The model also encourages us to invite some free-flowing, joyful spontaneity to keep the balance of energy moving through the behavioural quadrants, encouraging that positive energy to flow through the team, and the relationships between the individuals.

This essentially hopeful model imagines a workplace that is engaging and purposeful for all of us if we pay attention to our capacity for healthy and enjoyable human social functioning.

Summary

- Functional Fluency provides a framework for building constructive relationships at work.
- Effective behaviours can be chosen over ineffective ones, with self-awareness, the capacity to pause, and Account for the here-and-now reality.
- An effective manager knows the difference between reacting and responding.
- In a new role, all our relationships shift. These shifts need to be noticed and accounted for to accommodate the change.
- We bring assumptions to our leadership and management role. We can challenge these through the prism of reality checking (how useful/relevant are they now?) and make new choices.
- A functionally fluent leader learns and changes in response to their circumstances.
- Functionally fluent feedback is the bedrock skill of a constructive manager. It is useful, developmental, and clarifying. It provides motivation and direction too. Positive feedback is as important as challenging feedback for building effective working relationships.
- Healthy human social functioning at work benefits us all.

Notes

1 Adapted from "The Power of Choice", Temple, S.F. (2002).
2 CIPD (2012). *Managing for Sustainable Employee Engagement: guidance for employers and managers* [online]. London: Chartered Institute of Personnel and Development, p. 3, Table 1, Managing for sustainable engagement framework, available at https://www.cipd.co.uk/knowledge/fundamentals/relations/engagement/management-guide
3 Schmid, B. (2008). "The Role Concept of Transactional Analysis and other Approaches to Personality, Encounter, and Co-creativity for All Professional Fields", *Transactional Analysis Journal*, 38:1, 17–30, DOI: 10.1177/036215370803800104
4 Seligman, M. (2002). *Authentic Happiness*, Boston MA, USA, Nicholas Brealey Publishing.
5 Zenger, J. and Folkman, J. (2013). "The Ideal Praise-to-Criticism Ratio", *Harvard Business Review*: 15 March, 2013.
6 Hall, K. (2013). Making the Matrix Work: How Matrix Managers Engage People and Cut Through Complexity. London: Nicholas Brealey International.
7 Blake, R. and Mouton, J. (1964). *The Managerial Grid: The Key to Leadership Excellence.* Gulf Publishing, Houston Texas, USA.
8 Salovey, P. & Mayer, J.D. (1990). "Emotional Intelligence", *Journal of Imagination, Cognition and Personality*: Vol. 9 (3), pp. 185–211.
9 Goleman, D. (1995). *Emotional Intelligence*, Bantam Books.
10 Goleman, D., Boyatzis, R. and McKee, A. (2002). The New Leaders: Transforming the Art of Leadership into the Science of Results. London, Little & Brown (p. ix).

Chapter 4

The Inspirational Leader

Providing Vision and Purpose

Jutta Kreyenberg and Hannah Titilayo Seriki

Introduction

Climbing the hierarchical ladder in an organization is exciting and challenging. Step by step, you gain rank and importance. Your responsibility for others increases and your perspective changes. You begin to develop a birds-eye-view of the organization and its environment. The climb requires a significant amount of energy from you. Why do you do it?

It may be about making more money. It may be about being important and making big decisions. The adrenalin-rush of solving higher-level problems, and the fun of working with and harnessing the power of teams, may be what keeps you going. Or you may find that entering into a senior leadership position enables you to make a positive difference to society, and the world at large. Of course, there are infinite other possible reasons, big and small.

Beside your personal needs, wishes and dreams, directing your project, department or organization is central to your role as a project manager, middle-level manager, or executive manager. In this chapter, we concentrate on these roles, referring to them all as "senior leadership".

Only if you as the senior leader know where the journey is headed and why, can you inspire others to contribute their knowledge and expertise towards reaching this destination. Having said that, the person in charge rarely knows all the answers. This means that even while you as the senior leader are developing clarity about the direction of your enterprise, you are also involving and collaborating with others in your thought and decision-making processes. Senior leadership is not a role that you can take on as an isolated individual, but that is, at least to some extent, a role to be shared with others. While the senior leader will be privy to some important information, which those on other levels of the hierarchy do not have access to, other people may know more about specific operational details. The bigger, more complex or more distant your destination is, the more you will need to engage and inspire the experts who can provide whatever is needed for the many steps along the way.

DOI: 10.4324/9781003345527-4

Functional Fluency as an aid to choosing effective behaviours in inter-personal interactions is as valuable as ever. This chapter focusses especially on how Functional Fluency supports senior leaders in handling the following key leadership challenges:

Creating Vision & Purpose
Maintaining Role Clarity and Developing a Strategic Mindset
Developing Yourself and Others
Inspiring People

Creating vision and purpose

The Anglo-Saxon root of the word leadership is "laed", which means path or road. The verb, "laeden" means "to travel". Therefore, a leader can be seen as a sort of travel guide, who takes ideas, people, organizations, societies on a journey. On this journey, the leader articulates a vision, motivates and decides.[1]

This confirms what we already alluded to before – that leadership is not an activity that happens in isolation. A leader is always part of one (or several) systems, which he or she influences and is influenced by. The travel guide would not exist without the travellers and the environment within which the journey takes place.

Creating vision and purpose the Functional Fluency way includes sharing leadership, in the sense that more than one person is needed to articulate a vision, motivate and make decisions that move the system. How does this happen?

Our journey has a purpose when the *why* is clear. The central insight of Simon Sinek's Golden Circle Model[2] is that people do not buy into what you do, but why you do it. They are connected within the system by the purpose (consciously or not). If, as a senior leader, you talk about what you want to achieve, you will attract others with the same or similar desires. Those you work with will then not actually be sacrificing their energy for you as someone external to them, but for a shared purpose, which they are passionate about. This can make a big difference to people's motivation, and sense of responsibility and, as a consequence, influences people's ability and willingness to use the Golden Five (effective) behaviours described in the Functional Fluency model. Awareness and open communication of the journey's purpose enables senior leaders to inspire others, and to attract others who, in turn, inspire them.

"If you want to build a ship, don't drum up the men to gather wood, divide the work and give orders. Instead, teach them to yearn for the vast and endless sea."

(Antoine de Saint-Exupéry)

By rising up the ladder, senior leaders are more and more confronted with seemingly unsolvable problems and dilemmas, beginning with the challenge of optimizing cost, quality and speed at the same time, and ending with the disruption of entire markets. To deal with paradoxes and rapid changes, they need to acquire new Accounting skills. Their Accounting behaviours need to contain

- alertness to market and company stimuli
- building a new frame of reference
- viewing the organization and its environment from different angles
- staying grounded and authentic
- evaluating sustainability
- staying in contact with those who matter most: the people

Using the authoritative behaviour which is part of effective Structuring, you as the senior leader share what you know and do not know, your expertise and experience, developing trust through your authenticity. The "vast and endless sea" in the quote above represents whatever it is you are striving for with the organization that you are leading. You play with ideas, dream, allow your creativity to flow freely (Spontaneous). You talk about your dreams, experiments, insights, hypotheses, ... others, whose interest is aroused, listen. They add their own thoughts, opinions and experiences. You, interested in this as an addition to what you have come up with, listen (Cooperative), and a collaborative, innovative process has begun. This needs to be structured so as to continue and bear fruit in the long term. Structuring behaviours (in contrast to Dominating) will help you communicate the framework in which your "shipbuilding" needs to happen with clarity, authority and recognition of each party's ability to contribute – as opposed to just telling people what to do "because I say so". The collaborative approach and your own knowledge and enthusiasm will help to inspire others.

Accounting helps you evaluate collected information from different per-spectives. You can calculate the consequences that different choices for action will most probably have, and based on this you can make informed decisions.

The bond you have formed with other people in your system in the col-laborative process, in which people express what they think and feel (Spontaneous), where friendliness and assertiveness go hand in hand (Cooperative) paves the way for empathy and understanding. This helps you to recognize which needs must be fulfilled to nurture people and their project to their full potential (Nurturing).

Leading like this is more similar to developing a collective dance within a large, boundaried space than to marching in a straight line towards a fixed point.

Reflection

Think about your vision as a senior leader.

- What is your "vast and endless sea"?
- How have you enthused others to join you in building the ship to get you out there? Having read the section above, what do you think you can do to increase motivation and engagement within your workforce, keeping in mind the Golden Five behaviours?

As a senior leader you are in charge. Having established that this does not mean that you need to be an isolated dictator, it is useful to link what the Functional Fluency model teaches about Being in Charge to shared leadership and Nurturing culture. According to the Functional Fluency model, Being in Charge is about Guiding and Directing on the one hand and Caring for People on the other.

Sharing guidance and direction (Structuring all around)

As mentioned in earlier chapters explaining the Functional Fluency Model, effective Guiding and Directing includes setting goals, focusing on what is going well, offering challenges, sticking to clear limits, making agreements and saying when enough is enough. This is all part of Structuring behaviour. The effect is that help is given where needed, expectations are clear, standards are set and adhered to, and reliability is increased. The message sent to people is "You can do it!" Learning and empowerment are fostered.

If you are, for example, the CEO of a large multinational, it will be impossible for you to guide and direct each individual employee one-to-one. As you move up the hierarchy, your people, budget, and responsibility increase. You therefore need to become a leader of leaders and develop indirect leadership skills – your ability to lead through others. You can model the Structuring behaviours summarized above in leading a leadership team. A leadership team that is aligned around how to provide structure effectively can guide and direct the organization together. By modelling and sharing leadership, a senior leader fosters trust, facilitates agreement between colleagues on working methods and responsibilities, and develops a bonded leadership team, which has the strength to navigate through difficult times.

As a senior leader, you may use Structuring behaviour in a variety of ways. For example:

- Sounding out when projects and processes are not working, and acting to modify how things are done.
- Modelling a style of leadership of people that other leaders in your organization will feel inspired to emulate.

- Influencing the culture of the organization to be well-organized, authoritative, helpful and set boundaries which safeguard the organization's purpose and the ability of its people to fulfil that purpose.

Case study

Tim is an experienced senior leader with departmental responsibilities. The company recently repositioned itself, and is now working in the field of quality management/testing. The new focus is on customer acquisition/customer orientation. Tim was confronted with a high level of uncertainty and change during this time. This included changes in the leadership level above him, unrest in the management team (five department heads, many of whom lacked management skills and training), old reporting structures, and ways of working. A lot of clearing up was needed. Tim's Structuring activities to support leaders at his level and below included:

- getting a clear view of the business (this included asking questions and getting answers, if the direction was unclear), so that this could be clearly communicated to the next level
- reaching agreement on responsibilities and timelines with the levels above and below (target agreements)
- practising self-control (e.g. checking his own progress against set goals and making necessary adjustments)
- supporting Coaching/Mentoring of managers by the next higher level
- working with a documented business plan for his own department
- employee interviews to get insights from their perspective
- defining meeting agendas
- delegating tasks
- terminating contracts with those who could not fulfil the requirements

Developing a Nurturing culture within the organization is likely to complement the clear structure provided by the senior leader and their team.

Nurturing culture

Senior leaders can use their influence to contribute to the growth of the organization and individuals within it by forming and developing its culture.

The culture of an organization refers to what is valued, how things are done, the shared assumptions, beliefs and norms of the organization.

. This can include the Nurturing behaviours, which contribute to effective care. If offering warmth and appreciation, accepting people as they are, giving time and attention, listening with empathy, attempting to understand, and being available are "normal" behaviour in your organization, it is highly likely that your employees are healthy, motivated, and engaged.

Organizations are increasingly aware of the importance of employee engagement. This is about establishing mutual respect for what people can do and be, and is directly correlated to their performance. Senior leaders need to view the entire picture of strategy-system-culture with a focus on getting their people intrinsically involved. They need to see and understand the way people communicate in the company as a whole. Their task is not to "deal" with change, but to create and steer change[3]. Senior leaders steer the main factors for engagement in their company through:

- good quality line management
- intense and open two-way communication
- effective internal co-operation and teamwork
- a focus on development and learning
- commitment to employee well-being
- clear, accessible, HR policies and practices, to which managers at all levels are committed.[4]

Sometimes, leaders who mean well, and put a lot of energy into caring for people, can fall into the trap of exhibiting or promoting Marshmallowing (ineffective) behaviours instead of Nurturing (effective) ones.

Case study

For example, Anil led a large department of clinical teams within a health organization. He recognized the pressures everyone was working under, especially during the winter when there were added demands. Much of the time, Anil used appropriate Nurturing behaviours, empathizing with the difficulties team leaders were working with, and showing his understanding and compassion by checking out their needs, Accounting for the situations they were dealing with, and representing their needs to decision makers above him. However, his sense of responsibility started to extend to personally taking work off team leaders, and although they appreciated his concern for them, this started to make them feel they were losing status in the eyes of their teams, and that Anil was not trusting them to do their jobs. Anil was also failing to take breaks and often coming in on his day off, making his team leaders feel that this was expected of them too. His excellent Nurturing behaviours had slipped into Marshmallowing, smothering others, giving them the message that he didn't think they were good enough.

Developing a caring culture in an organization is something anyone can do if they make it a priority. The creation of such a culture can be hugely beneficial for everyone – provided it is "effective" care (Nurturing). The enabling mentality of Structuring is then complemented by the accepting and understanding mentality of Nurturing. Assuming that your vision and purpose are clear, this combination of attitudes behind your actions will help attract and retain people who share your vision and purpose. It also provides you and your people with a safe space in which to build your ship – together.

Collaborating as a senior leader – The Golden blend

For those senior leaders who have a project management role, leading cross-organizational projects such as system innovation and consistency or global reach, functionally fluent leadership provides effectiveness without the authority of line management. These senior leaders need to be able to move fluently between Accounting, Structuring, Nurturing, Cooperative, and Spontaneous behaviours.

Case study

Sara was tasked with leading a project to ensure that the IT systems required by different parts of her organization could work together, and take full advantage of technical innovations being introduced by her colleagues. At first, she tried talking to managers in each department about why the organization needed them to comply, and asking them to report to her on what they were doing to ensure this would happen in their part of the organization. However, she soon discovered that giving her the information she needed was low on their lists of priorities. They were much more interested in putting their energies into actions which would fulfil their departmental goals than her project goals.

After learning about Functional Fluency, Sara realized that she needed to use a more Cooperative approach, discuss with each department their current concerns and future needs (with empathy and understanding) and then show them through Structuring (well-organized, authoritative, helpful and inspiring) and Cooperative behaviour, how her project could ensure that their current efforts were future proofed, and would enable them to reach their goals. She had changed a command-and-control approach, which came across to others as Dominating, to an influencing approach using effective behaviours.

This style of working is also required in matrix management systems, where senior leaders at the top of organizations may set goals but may not have the experience, skills or knowledge to determine how they are reached.[5] "Eye-level" leadership is particularly needed here, meaning that senior leaders at different levels work together with their peers while simultaneously managing subordinates, and fulfilling requirements of those above them. The skills represented by functionally fluent communication are vital for collaboration in the matrix to be effective. Also, those who are faced with the demands of meeting targets and deadlines in a hierarchical structure can easily forget the value of collaboration across peer groups.

Reflection

Think about the culture of your organization.

- What are "normal" behaviours?
- What is the balance of Structuring, Nurturing, Cooperative, Spontaneous, Accounting?
- Does Dominating, Marshmallowing, Compliant/Resistant or Immature behaviour also feature in your organizational culture? How could you transform this into more effective patterns?

Maintaining role clarity and developing a strategic mindset

Understanding your role remains vital as your leadership responsibility increases. It can be useful to revisit the multi-world-view, which was introduced as Bernd Schmid's 3-world view in Chapter 3 (The Constructive Manager). This was later expanded by Günther Mohr to include the world of society. Since this is especially relevant to senior leaders, this chapter refers to the 4-world model.

Taking into account the senior leader's varied roles

As a senior leader, your main challenge is how to really get behind the steering wheel of the organizational world, and integrate all the worlds in which you operate into an understanding of yourself as a person, and as a part of the organization. Your lens of awareness as a senior leader becomes wider than it was before – more very different aspects of your inner and outer reality are included in your Accounting.

For first level managers, developing leadership attitudes and abilities is a major challenge as well as an interesting developmental journey. Bernd Schmid's 3-world model[6], which was introduced in the last chapter, describes "three worlds" which contain different role sets, defined as the expectations of significant others towards a certain social position, e.g. people's expectations towards "a mother", "a manager", "an engineer", "a voluntary sports coach" etc. Each role includes thinking, feeling, behaviour, and the shaping of relationships. This is not about acting out roles but about developing oneself in an integrated way in and across the different worlds. The higher you climb on the hierarchical ladder, the more influence you gain, and the more relevant it becomes to add the world of society[7] to the other three worlds mentioned before. It is especially important for senior leaders to take into account the role of the company within society.

Human beings start their journey of life in the private world, which includes the roles of child, mother, father, friends etc. By choosing a profession, becoming an apprentice, or studying and beginning to work in our first job, we start to work, think, and feel as a professional (e.g. engineer, salesperson etc.). When someone enters into a leadership position for the first time, the organizational world changes for them. Because of the different roles and mindsets, the transition from one world to the other involves conflict, tension and mistakes. This is why the leader's personal development journey is so important.

While the focus of a first-time manager is on entering into and accepting the role of leader, saying goodbye to the original, more task-oriented occupation, by contrast the changes for senior leaders are often more subtle. The 4-world model, as shown in Figure 4.1, with its additional systemic perspective, highlights that leadership is not only about the person but also about the interaction, the culture, structure, and strategy of the organization as well as its influences on the market, and the connection to societal issues such as environmental impact or contribution to overcoming current problems

Figure 4.1 The 4-world-model adapted from Mohr (2008).[7]

(like floods, a pandemic, social inequality, racism etc.). The strategic view, that the senior leader develops, extends the view from the organization further out into society. Thus, the role of senior leader highlights responsibility outside the organization as well as inside it.

From the grounded and logical position of Accounting, senior leaders need to learn to prioritize their roles in the organizational world and, zooming out to a higher level of understanding, to integrate the roles they hold in all four worlds. This includes coping with the following issues and their inherent dilemmas:

- *Business:* What is the context of the organization (e.g. markets, industry)
- *Structure:* How is the organization structured (e.g. classical, agile, how much digitalization)?
- *Vision:* What is the organization's vision and, based on this, the strategy in the short and long term?
- *Culture:* How can the company's culture be described and how do we develop/maintain it?
- *Society:* How do we contribute meaning to the world around us?

The senior leader needs to focus on the surviving and thriving of the company as a whole. Your focus is not on individual members, but on the structure, culture, and strategy of the organization. You need a lot of experience and the ability to think systemically about how things influence each other to find second-order solutions.

Developing a strategic mindset

All this means that being a senior leader includes taking full responsibility for the organization with its people, within its context, and acting from the attitude of executive instead of employee. This requires even more pro-activity or, in Functional Fluency terms, increased ability to respond to challenges with the situationally appropriate use of all Golden Five effective behaviours. To use a metaphor, you need to be in the driving seat, rather than being driven.

Communication is a strategic activity at the senior leadership level. The Functional Fluency map can help the leader to get clarity about communication needs at different levels:

- Structuring: Who needs to receive which information when, in what level of detail, through which channels?
- Nurturing: Are you observing and listening in such a way that you can pick up information, views and concerns from your stakeholders (internal and external) that may impact the organization in the short or long term?
- Cooperative: Are the conversations you are having with stakeholders fostering cooperation?

- Spontaneous: Are you still imagining possibilities and expressing your ideas? Who can you do this best with? Which people or groups can take this further?

Case study

Frank, who was promoted from the middle management position of a plant leader to a senior position of department head, reported directly to the board and was responsible for 10 plants all over Europe. At first, Frank tried to manage every plant like he had managed his home plant, including regular one-to-ones with individual employees, detailed problem-solving discussions, and communication to the board regarding each plant. He was soon overwhelmed by the number of tasks and expectations, could no longer sleep, got severe headaches and finally, failing to cope with the new challenge, ended up with burnout. The insights Functional Fluency gave him helped him to see that he had been doing the job of all the plant managers on top of his own. While meaning to take care of people, he had attempted to do it all for them, which led to confusion about roles and frustration as a reaction to the message he was unconsciously sending out to his subordinates – "You are inadequate". Frank had failed to gain role clarity or adopt a strategic mindset and was using Marshmallowing behaviours.

When he realized this, he could begin to deal with his own stress and accept his own human limitations (Nurturing toward self). He then set the right focus. He developed confidence in himself as a leader and established what his plant teams actually needed from him to reach their goals. He overcame his anxiety-driven behaviours like doing other people's jobs for them, and let go of self-denying behaviours in which he overindulged the people around him. He no longer confused needs and wants. Frank also learned to negotiate resources in an assertive way, which meant that he could support all the plants he was responsible for in getting their jobs done without having to go into nitty-gritty operational details with them. His work-life balance was re-established and so was that of his teams. Less overtime, surprisingly to Frank at first, led to higher productivity, and less sick leave. A nice side-effect for Frank was that people respected and trusted him a lot more than they had before, especially when they learned about some of the personal difficulties he overcame.

Table 4.1 summarizes the main challenges in proceeding as a leader to higher levels, the contribution of Functional Fluency and the learning needs of the developing leader.

Table 4.1 Contributions of Functional Fluency at different levels of management

Focus	First-level management	Senior leadership — Middle management	Senior team
Key challenges	• new relationships • clear definition of roles • team development • digital leadership • delivering bad news	• leading change • aligning leaders • dealing with conflicts • first structural interventions • tactical communication	• building a leadership team • restructuring • dealing with uncertainty, ambiguity, complexity, paradoxes • closing the dialogue gap bottom up
Functional Fluency Some key contributions	• combining Structuring and Nurturing to engage and support staff to achieve goals and develop • Cooperative behaviour to support effective interaction with peers, superiors and employees • using Accounting to increase awareness of multiple factors in management issues and causes of stress	• Structuring to prioritize and organize what needs to get done by whom and when • Nurturing to contribute to healthy caring culture and respond to own stress levels • using and encouraging Cooperative behaviour at team and departmental level	• using Accounting to stay aware of all possible influences on the organization and to consciously choose effective behaviours • Nurturing self and others to maintain healthy energy levels • Structuring self and others to maintain clarity, focus and sense of responsibility • Cooperating with colleagues in shared leadership wherever that contributes to goal setting and achievement
	• Spontaneous behaviour to express observations, feelings and ideas appropriately across hierarchical levels		
Leadership development and learning needs	• authentic communication at all levels • getting things done • understanding of roles, focus on the organizational role • taking a more objective point of view	• shifting the focus from operative to strategic systemic thinking • letting go of direct control • fostering performance through clear objectives • identifying values and motivators	• leading leaders • integrating tactical and political management with authenticity • shared leadership • self-management

Developing yourself and others

Leading ourselves effectively is the first important step to take towards developing the ability to lead others well. Self-development and self-leadership, through the Functional Fluency lens, is not about changing your personality or character. It is rather about developing personal maturity through awareness of your own behavioural patterns, the stories behind them, and the effects on you and those you are in contact with. You can develop your awareness for the choices you make, the thinking, feeling and behaviours you use to influence the world around you. If a situation is not ideal, you can complain and suffer, or you can do something about it!

Developing yourself means enlarging your options to reach your goals, and overcome impediments like fear and stress. This can only come through self-reflection, which over time becomes habitual for anyone committed to developing themselves further.

Reflection

There are a couple of key questions that may help you reflect on and get feedback about how functionally fluent you currently are with your leadership actions:

•   What mindset/beliefs about yourself and others are your actions based on?
•   Are you empowering or disempowering people through what you do?

The first challenge is to be absolutely honest and compassionate with yourself as you answer these questions. As you practise leading yourself, you develop the capacity to recognize learning possibilities in all your experiences, be they comfortable or challenging. You learn to consciously decide what you do, and if everyone continues to develop positively because of what you are doing, you are being effective.

How do you achieve this? Effective behaviour usually begins with Accounting. As a senior leader you take into account your own strengths and weaknesses, resources, obstacles, likes and dislikes and what is truly important to you (your values). Based on this, you can dive into

•   planning and developing the way towards the big goal (Structuring)
•   recognizing what you personally need in order to make it, and ensure you get this (Nurturing)
•   liaising with others to run different parts of the endeavour (Cooperating)
•   and tapping into your own unique talent and passion (Spontaneous).

As a senior leader who is strengthening these behavioural patterns for yourself, you are developing your own capacity for self-reflection, and it is likely that your behaviour will inspire others to develop this capacity for themselves, too. Leadership development and, more generally, personal development is an inward process as well as an outward one. As Stephen Covey points out, "To try to change outward attitudes and behaviours does very little good in the long run if we fail to examine the basic paradigms from which those attitudes and behaviours flow."[8]

So, developing a flexible combination of the Golden Five behaviours in your interpersonal interactions will be based on continuous explorations and adaptations of your beliefs about yourself and other people. Remaining conscious and honest about this is no easy feat, especially when the pressure is on!

Case study

Pietro was the relatively new CEO of an organization providing social services. He was appointed to grow the service and was offered a large new contract, involving taking on more clients, more staff, and changing the way the organization operated. His management team had been very resistant to change. They argued that they were overloaded, and his belief that they would not be accepting of his ideas meant that he avoided talking to them about the changes he had been appointed to make.

In discussion with a coach, Pietro thought through possible objections which he believed would be raised at a coming meeting to introduce the new contract. In considering what the management team needed from him, Pietro at first thought only of what they would refuse to do, or ask him to do. Gradually, he considered how he could help get them on board. He planned possible answers and reassurances for their objections, and with the help of Functional Fluency, also looked at how he could develop the management team's involvement by showing that he valued their experience and views (Nurturing), and appealing to their values (inspiring). Instead of presenting the contract as extra work which would disrupt the usual way of working, this was an opportunity for them to deliver a much-needed new service to clients they cared about. The meeting went much more smoothly than he had been fearing. Pietro reported that it helped him to see how to use a more collaborative approach, and empower others, to facilitate others to use their experience and understanding to feel involved in the decisions, instead of imposing decisions because he was afraid of the response he believed he would get.

Dealing with stress and ineffective behaviours

While you may aspire to use the constructive energy of the Golden Five be-havioural modes as much as possible, it is also crucial to recognize what triggers you to use the less effective behaviours, your own typical Purple Pitfalls.

Unfortunately, leadership effectiveness frequently decreases with the hier-archical rank of the leader instead of increasing.[9] Why could this be happening?

Senior leaders are often under a lot of personal stress and receive very little personal feedback from others. This can make it harder, instead of easier, for a senior leader to engage in reflective processes, and develop the emotional intelligence and interactive leadership skills that are required if they are to succeed in the senior leadership role. Personal development and behavioural change do not happen in defined steps. It can be quite an un-certain journey, on which the senior leader has to bear a lot of not-knowing and needs feedback and support from others along the way. Simply ac-knowledging this as a fact can be valuable to any senior leader. It clarifies why stress and isolation are factors that hinder personal and organizational growth. No wonder stressed senior leaders are repeatedly seen to exhibit Purple Pitfall behaviour, like bossiness or immature shouting.

The insights in Chapter 5, which focusses on developing resilience, will shed some more light on how to deal with stressful situations, overcome them, and strengthen your ability to respond (consciously) rather than react (automatically).

Case studies

Mary used to be a kind and attentive team leader, popular and liked by her team members. When she rose into a senior management role, her social behaviour went increasingly "purple". On a personal profile providing a snapshot of her behaviour in Functional Fluency terms (TIFF – Temple Index of Functional Fluency)[10] her Dominating behaviour scores were high, showing her tendencies to fault-finding and punitive behaviours. The profile also indicated a pattern of acting in a Compliant way when overwhelmed. She recognized that her anxiety about failing, and her struggle to meet everybody's demands led to her other ineffective behaviours, especially Dominating ones. Some of her employees fed back to her that they observed her becoming erratic and unpredictable, sometimes even unapproachable, and absent in her leadership approach. She definitely did not want to have that effect on her people. So, her first step was to realign herself to her needs and find better ways of dealing with the stress. She especially worked on letting go of the tendency to try to "please others". Learning to trust herself, and taking her own position was key for her. Only after this step was she able to restructure her work, and find new, different ways to communicate with her leadership team and start the team alignment process.

Another example is John, whose personal profile showed higher scores for Immature than for Spontaneous behaviours. When his coach asked what this could mean for him, he mentioned having a disabled daughter and a highly stressful management job with immense responsibility. For him, life was all work and no fun. From time to time, he ignored all his responsibilities, went on a wild motorcycle ride or a drinking binge. Fortunately, not both together!

Functional Fluency provided both Mary and John with a framework for moving away from the Purple Pitfalls they were stuck in. This process began with Accounting – asking themselves what was actually going on, and exploring how they could change their situations by making different behavioural choices. They needed to recognize their own need for development before they could begin to do anything about increasing their leadership effectiveness towards others. Wise and efficient Accounting makes leaders suitably "with-it", for instance by good boundary keeping, timing, and choice of methods and strategies for the leadership process.

The Structuring and Nurturing behaviours are empowering. Instead of shouting at or threatening her employees (Dominating), Mary set out clear expectations, guidelines, time frames, and communication structures for her teams, which helped them organize work among themselves, and realize early enough if they needed extra information or resources to get tasks done. The fact that Mary took these needs into account as a leader and made sure they were met (Nurturing), if she knew about it on time, further contributed to the empowerment of others.

John needed to admit his own needs in supporting himself. Finding a coach was the first step out if his personal Purple Pitfall. He began to use Nurturing behaviour towards himself.

Cooperative and Spontaneous modes engender potency. When Mary opened herself up to conversations with her employees, was able to listen to their feedback, accept it and explain what she needed from them (Cooperative), she was able to truly step into her power as a leader. The "Fun Feedback Fridays" she later initiated in her organization were inspired by her love of stories and storytelling, which she used as a medium to facilitate the expression of feelings and observations in a non-threatening way. (Spontaneous).

John still needs an outlet for all his pent-up energy, and still enjoys riding his motorbike along winding mountain roads. These excursions help him breathe, and he realizes how important it is for him to do something just because he enjoys it so much – while at the same time exercising appropriate caution to minimize the danger of being injured or injuring others. Instead of binge-drinking, he'll meet up with supportive, understanding friends for a drink and a chat, or go trail-running as an outlet to frustration and tension. He usually comes back calmer (sober but inspired) with a new perspective and new ideas.

Reflection

1   Remember a time when you felt stressed, pressured or lonely in your senior leadership role.

- What physical sensations do you recall?
- What did you do in reaction to this?
- What were your Purple Pitfalls?
- What happened next?

2   Remember a time when you felt confident and positive in your senior leadership role.

- What physical sensations do you recall?
- How did you interact with and empower others from this state?
- What were the (positive) outcomes?

3   In preparation for your next stressful situation

- What will you be more aware of to avoid the Purple Pitfalls from above?
- What will help you tap into the resources that were available to you in the positive example above?

Inspiring people

As the title of this chapter suggests, senior leadership is essentially about inspiring people.

Inspiration is defined as "the process of being mentally stimulated to do or feel something, especially something creative".[11] This is exactly what this chapter has been about – developing leadership behaviours that get people emotionally involved with a larger purpose, that empower people, energize them and stimulate their own creative processes.

Daniel Goleman points out that as the business world reinvents itself at immense speed, what makes leaders effective has been transformed and that "The New Leader" excels in the art of relationship, inspiring people by articulating a purpose which attunes with people's own values.[12] This chapter has highlighted the interpersonal skills mapped out by Functional Fluency as a guide to leadership effectiveness, with inspiration as a central theme.

Within the Functional Fluency Model, "inspiring" is one of the terms used to describe the Structuring behaviours. In this context "inspiring" also means (similar to the dictionary definition above) "exciting and encouraging someone to do or feel something". In addition to that "breathing life into"; "energizing", "enabling", "demonstrating passion" are noted by the originator of Functional Fluency as elements of being "inspiring".

There are many things that the inspirational leader does to inspire. A checklist for this would include much of what you have just read in this chapter about

> Creating Vision & Purpose
> Developing Yourself and Others
> Maintaining Role Clarity and Developing a Strategic Mindset

We believe that a more encompassing list of behaviours will not add much to your development as an inspirational leader. Reading explanations and case studies may have nudged you into thinking about this. We assume that remembering the people who have truly inspired you will add a lot of value for your next steps.

Reflection

- Who are the people who have inspired you?
- What did they do?
- How did they make you feel?
- What action did you take as a result?
- Can you follow their example and still be authentically yourself?

As an inspirational leader, you breathe life into your organization, not only by what you do, but also by who you are and what you believe in. In our search to understand what people find inspiring in their leaders, we found that the actions of inspiring leaders can be very diverse. What inspirational leaders seem to have in common is that they know and talk about their values, they know and build on their strengths, and they are able to remain calm under stress – centred in Accounting, the heart of Functional Fluency.

Summary

In summary, the following points characterize the Inspirational Leader:

- they recognize that they are part of the systems they are aiming to shape, and collaborate with others in articulating a vision, motivating people and making decisions that move the system

- they develop a culture of "effective" care (Nurturing) in their organization signalling to people "You're OK as you are!", which they complement with the "You can do it!" of Structuring action
- they maintain clarity on their role, develop a strategic mindset and become increasingly proactive as responsibility increases
- they take time to reflect on and develop themselves, constantly growing awareness for their own behavioural patterns, the stories behind them, and the consequences that result from them, gaining maturity and choices
- they know their triggers, and have learnt to deal with stress constructively
- they are open to inspiration from others, are grounded in themselves, and show up authentically as the inspirational leader they are

Notes

1 Adler, N. J. (2002) International Dimensions of Organizational Behaviour, fourth edition. Cincinnati Ohio: South-Western College Publishing.
2 Sinek, S. (2009) Start with why – how great leaders inspire everyone to take action. New York: Portfolio.
3 Robinson, D et al. (2004) *The Drivers of Employee Engagement Report 408*. UK: Institute for Employment Studies.
4 Robinson, D et al. (2004) *The Drivers of Employee Engagement Report 408*. UK: Institute for Employment Studies.
5 Hall, K. (2013) Making the Matrix Work: how matrix managers engage people and cut through complexity. London: John Murray Press.
6 Schmidt, B. Das Drei-Welten-Modell der Persönlichkeit. Available at https:// bibliothek.isb-w.eu/alfresco/d/d/workspace/SpacesStore/601767f8–64fa-40fc-9fcd-459c9315293e/015_das_drei-welten-modell.pdf
7 Mohr, G. (2008) Coaching und Selbstcoaching mit Transaktionsanalyse. EHP Praxis.
8 Covey, S (2004) The 7 Habits of Highly Effective People – Restoring the Character Ethic. New York: Free Press.
9 Wright, T. (2016) *The Functionally Fluent Organisation – 2016 Update*. Available at https://www.scribd.com/document/456195617/The-Functionally-Fluent-Organisation-2016-Update
10 More information about the TIFF personal profiling tool for Functional Fluency is given in the Appendix.
11 Online Dictionary. Available at: https://www.lexico.com/definition/inspiration
12 Goleman, D. Boyatzis, R & McKee, A. (2002) The New Leaders – Transforming the Art of Leadership into the Science of Results. London: Little, Brown.

Chapter 5

Building Your Personal Resilience with Functional Fluency

David Scott Brown

Introduction

The workplace is a dynamic environment. Against this backdrop you may be flourishing in a junior management position, or making a big splash running your own small business. Perhaps you're a department head, a recently promoted middle manager, or a CEO in the charity sector. Whatever your role, as the person in charge, your work can be both exciting and stimulating. Helping to shape the direction of your organization, developing the people within it, and making the decisions that matter, can be highly rewarding and a source of great job satisfaction.

But what if things aren't going well? What if you have the growing sense that there is a price to pay for keeping on top of your workload? Perhaps you are beginning to feel tired more often, or your ability to think clearly has deserted you? It could be that you've begun to snap at staff, or your relationships at home are under strain? Maybe you feel more anxious than you used to, you're sleeping less soundly, and you're constantly putting decision-making on hold? If this sounds like you, Functional Fluency can help you gain control, perform more effectively, and boost your personal resilience.

What is personal resilience?

It is often thought that being resilient means you must 'tough it out', keep your feelings to yourself, and maintain what the British call 'the stiff upper lip'. This, however, is only part of the story. Whilst personal resilience does indeed embrace qualities of mental toughness, and the ability to bounce back when things go wrong, other factors also contribute to this. Resilience is a strength, an attitude and a set of skills which can be learned. This is a cause for optimism because if you work at improving your resilience, you will get better at leading and managing. Instead of taking things personally or becoming hi-jacked by fear, you can develop greater confidence and a new zest for work.

DOI: 10.4324/9781003345527-5

Karen Reivich, co-director of the *Penn Resiliency Project*, maintains that resilience is the ability to 'adapt and persevere when things go awry'[1]. This notion of adaptability, alongside the capacity for change, is likewise emphasized by Jenny Campbell in *The Resilience Dynamic*[2]. As well as noting the need for flexibility and adaptability, however, Campbell points to a synergistic link between resilience and wellbeing. As she puts it, 'If you invest in your wellbeing, you are investing in your resilience, and vice versa. Resilience encompasses and indeed leverages wellbeing.'

Whilst change and uncertainty are inevitable at work, you can learn to flex and adapt, choosing to respond rather than react in challenging situations. You can become self-aware and can learn to tune into your emotions, using these to guide your decision-making. Instead of feeling like the stuffing has been knocked out of you, this improved self-awareness will reinvigorate you, contribute to a greater sense of wellbeing, and allow you to direct your energy towards positive outcomes for all.

Resilient leaders and managers put themselves in the best position to thrive in any circumstances. They invest in their personal development and appreciate that the things they do impact their relationships with colleagues, as well as the success of their organization. Just as importantly, however, they can take a step back to reflect inwardly, understanding how their thoughts and feelings shape their personal health outcomes. They realize that by enhancing their own sense of wellbeing, they can improve their effectiveness at work and beyond.

Engaging with Functional Fluency promotes increased resilience. The Functional Fluency Model provides a powerful framework that will enable you to take responsibility for managing yourself, to grow in confidence, and to perform at your optimum level more often. By using Functional Fluency to enhance your self-awareness, you will be able to identify where you are less effective. Your unhelpful, albeit very human, behaviours are likely to drain rather than boost your energy and can make you feel worn out rather than up for the next challenge. Happily, by practising Functional Fluency, you are also practising using behaviours that contribute to greater resilience. It's a win-win.

Why your 'survival instinct' may be letting you down

As one of the people who calls the shots, you will face many situations that will test you. On bad days, for example, you may find yourself constantly questioning your decisions, or worse, wondering whether this is the job for you. Being resilient does not mean shying away from this truth, but neither does it mean opting out of confronting the issues that need to be addressed. Rather, it means accepting the sometimes-turbulent nature of your work and having strategies that ensure you are more likely to be effective in spite of this. Being able to orchestrate these strategies on a consistent basis depends on modifying your unhelpful behaviours, and there are solid evolutionary reasons why this can be challenging.

Whenever you are confronted with a difficult or stressful situation, your body tries to help you by activating a stress response. Information is sent to the amygdalae, two bundles of nerve cells, one in each hemisphere of the brain. One job of the amygdalae is to interpret the sensory information your brain receives in the form of sounds and images, and to send a signal to the hypothalamus, the brain's command centre, which communicates with the rest of the body via the autonomic nervous system. The stress hormones, adrenaline and cortisol, are then pumped into your bloodstream, causing changes in your body as a 'sympathetic' response is activated.

Whilst 'sympathetic' may seem an odd word to describe a reaction that can feel so uncomfortable, the fact is that your body is preparing to keep you safe. The racing heartbeat, as blood is pushed to your muscles and vital organs, is perfectly normal when you are reacting to a potentially dangerous situation. Other symptoms include rapid breathing and a heightened sense of alertness, the feeling of being 'on edge'. You may become hypervigilant as the extra oxygen that has been delivered to your brain sharpens your senses in the face of what, based on your reactions in potentially similar past situations you perceive as a threat. This evolutionary response is designed to ensure your survival, but there is a problem: your body doesn't realize that you are only going about your job, and in most cases, this doesn't usually put you in real, physical danger.

Human beings experience negative emotions in many situations, but what you do with these emotions is key. The 'fight, flight or freeze' reaction is deeply embedded in all of us, but you can learn to overcome it wherever it is not serving you well. Today, it is no longer necessary to defend yourself against predators such as the sabre-toothed cat, *Dinofelis*. Rather, the 'adversary' you are likely to be facing is the team member who disagrees with a decision you have made, the angry customer on the other end of the phone, or the depressed set of monthly figures. These, too, might send stress hormones coursing wildly through your body, but given the reality of the situation, this is usually inappropriate and unhelpful. It is your behaviour that counts when your buttons have been pressed. Choose more effective behaviours more often, and over time you boost your personal resilience.

With Functional Fluency, you can learn to remain in control of your responses in spite of uncertainty, and to behave in ways which will elicit greater benefits for yourself and others. Within the drama of the work environment, when things go wrong and problems arise, you can learn to maintain a sense of proportion, and might even discover that you are able to thrive under pressure. You can create greater impact, not by controlling others, but by positively influencing them through managing yourself. In fact, by becoming aware of your own non-resilient behaviours, and by using resilient ones more often, you will be able to drop the struggle, and focus on developing your ability to use your energy more effectively. As a result, you will be effective in a wider range of situations, and when you are not, you will be able to diagnose the reasons for this and put things right.

True, there are times when the emotions you experience may be so powerful that there seems little you can do to control your reactions. And yet, recent advances in neuroscience have demonstrated that you do, in fact, have a choice about how to deal with the everyday issues you encounter. If, in such situations, you use ineffective behaviours, it's no longer accurate, when excusing yourself for these behaviours, to argue, 'that's just the way I am.' Brain scan imagery demonstrating the plasticity of the brain, can now reveal that such a statement is outdated.

Neuroplasticity, the process by which you really can change the physical structure of your brain, and therefore your habitual ineffective behaviours, should give you cause for optimism. It is amazing, and yet absolutely true, that by using Functional Fluency, you really do have the power to install brand new neural pathways into your brain, and as a result, you can learn to do things differently. You no longer need to be at the mercy of behaviours which were 'programmed in' decades ago, usually during childhood.

Indeed, it may now be more accurate to remind yourself of your status as a 'human becoming' rather than a human being. By this, I mean that you can legitimately feel encouraged by the idea that though this is the person you have become, given your experiences so far, the real truth is that by practising Functionally Fluent behaviours, you can reshape your future, and become the leader or manager you would love to be.

The central role of Accounting in building personal resilience

Taking your first steps

> *Everything can be taken from a man but one thing: the last of the human freedoms – to choose one's attitude in any given set of circumstances, to choose one's own way* (Victor E. Frankl)[3]

Dr. Victor Frankl arrived at this important insight whilst imprisoned in Auschwitz and other concentration camps during the Second World War. Made to endure horrific treatment at the hands of the Nazis, Frankl came to understand that no matter the circumstances that face us, we always have a choice in how we respond. Moment by moment, you can exercise that choice, even though the things that happen to you may be outside your control. In choosing to respond more effectively, you can positively influence the outcome, and certainly feel better about any situation with which you are confronted.

The positive choices you make at work are a result of effective internal processing, known as *intrapersonal effectiveness*. However, many of us, particularly when under stress, can attach negative meanings to the situations we encounter. For this reason, it is important to understand that meaning making is an active process; in other words, you alone create the thinking which ultimately shapes the experiences you have. If you indulge yourself in thoughts which make you feel frustrated, it may not be entirely your 'fault' if you scream at a customer, or make colleagues feel uncomfortable by slamming your folders on the desk. But don't expect others to see it this way.

Your patterns of thought, and the feelings you experience as a result of your thinking, are often so ingrained that they seem to happen automatically, but to be effective in your role, you need to take complete responsibility for them. Your thoughts and feelings, whether helpful or unhelpful, fuel your behaviours, and for this reason, in a very real sense, they directly influence your interactions with others. You were introduced to this idea in The Power of Choice diagram in Chapters 2 and 3. To enhance your *interpersonal effectiveness,* it is useful to take time to uncover your unhelpful thinking patterns and to replace them with more helpful ones. Doing so is a hallmark of resilience and can be practised by using Functional Fluency. The following activity will enable you to begin that process:

Reflection: Changing unhelpful thinking patterns

1   Think of a stressful situation that occurs at work, such as not having enough time, or finding a person difficult to deal with. Try to identify the feelings you experience in this situation.

2   What is your internal dialogue when you think about this? In other words, what do you say to yourself? Examples might be, 'I'll let everyone down' or 'This person is impossible.'

3   What kind of thinking have you identified? Do your thoughts match up with any of the rules you have about yourself, or about the world? For example, 'I mustn't make a mistake', or 'People shouldn't let me down.'

4   Consider other situations in your life where you unconsciously react to your *shoulds* and *musts.*

5   Rewrite your rules, taking out the 'all or nothing' aspects. A more helpful and realistic rule to use in situations such as that highlighted in the example above, where you are tempted to tell yourself that you mustn't make mistakes, could be, 'As a human being, I am bound to make *some* mistakes, but I don't have to let those mistakes define me, or stop me from behaving more effectively in future.' Learn your new rules by heart, and practise using them whenever you face challenging situations which in the past might not have turned out well.

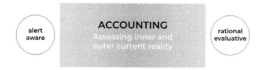

Figure 5.1 Accounting.

Accounting for situations

In Chapter 2, you learned about Accounting (see Figure 5.1 here), and discovered that it is a set of internal processes which you can use to make sense of what is going on. Moment by moment, as a leader or manager, you will face situations which have the potential to challenge your resilience, and therefore your sense of wellbeing. Using internal energy effectively means deciding what you need to take account of in the here and now. Effective Accounting gives you control of your response, and restores clarity of thought. The more Accounting you do, the more fluent you become at doing it.

Reflection: Creating negative emotions

Close your eyes and imagine an incident from the past when things didn't go well for you at work; a time when, perhaps, everything felt like a struggle, and where now, looking back, you are aware of having reacted unhelpfully to the challenge that faced you. This may link to the situation you considered in the previous Reflection but could be an entirely different example. If so far, everything at work has gone well, try to think of an incident from your personal life that was similarly challenging, and where, perhaps, you lost a little of your usual sense of self-control. As you conjure up that moment, can you recall how you behaved, how effective or ineffective your behaviours were, and how others reacted to you?

As mentioned earlier, with your thoughts come feelings and emotions, so as you brought to mind this experience, you may have found yourself feeling anxious, or possibly angry or fearful. If so, take a deep breath, then reassure yourself with the fact that, like the rest of us, you are a human being with uniquely human emotions.

It's worth pointing out here, that your brain can do amazing things. Even though you haven't moved from the comfort of your chair (assuming you are sitting in a chair), in effect, you have travelled back in time and not just experienced, but actually recreated, the thoughts and feelings associated with something that happened to you in the past. And yet, here you are, safe in this moment. As you will discover below, this moment-by-moment understanding of what is real in the here and now, as opposed to what you imagine about the past or the future, is crucial to making Functional Fluency work for you.

An Accounting process for assessing inner and outer reality when facing challenge

Below are some possible Accounting responses which may prove more effective than simply lashing out, running away, or alternatively, freezing, and doing nothing in the face of challenge.

- *Alert*: Firstly, it is important to celebrate the fact that you have recognized why you feel like reacting in the first place. This already puts you in a position to begin making sense of the situation.
- *Aware*: You switch on to the processes taking place inside your body, as well as to what is going on 'out there'. For example, you may think that the team member who has complained about a gossipy colleague should just ignore them, but if they aren't happy with your response, you have a problem. In a different scenario, you might become alert to your tendency to be harsh with yourself about something you have done. Alternatively, being alert may help you realize that you are actually preventing yourself from doing something because you are telling yourself that you are not good enough. You may notice your heartbeat speeding up and your breathing becoming shallow (see above). Accounting for and monitoring your physiological response enhances the likelihood of a more beneficial outcome, so you could take some deep breaths to help reinstate a feeling of calm.
- *Grounded*: Using grounded behaviours means paying attention to the reality of the present moment, remaining 'present' and balanced. Colloquially, it is about keeping both feet planted firmly on the ground. As you pay attention to this moment and become more aware of the ways you may habitually react based on patterns from the past, you can decide, in this instance, to respond, knowing that doing so is likely to benefit everyone.
- *Evaluative*: It is important to weigh things up, and to remind yourself that in the here and now, your body believes it is under attack, whereas in fact, you are perfectly safe. You might also mentally interrogate the truth, or otherwise, of your beliefs. For example, you might realize the unhelpfulness of expressing your opinion which, after all, is simply that. Just because *you* think that the complainant should ignore the office bully, doesn't make it true. Evaluation might also include exploring what is going on in a situation so that you can use this full knowledge in the choices you make. For example, a staff member who is unusually defensive or angry may be reacting to something else that has happened to them today of which you are unaware.

- *Enquiring*: In order to make full sense of a situation, you may need to investigate further by asking questions as a means to seek understanding and to establish fact from opinion, or indeed to challenge your own thinking or way of seeing things.
- *Rational*: Finally, with practice over time, you can learn to think more logically in the moment, using reason, as well as the facts you gathered when using enquiring behaviours. This is the case no matter what unhelpful patterns you have adopted in the past, and each time you practise, you become more fluent at keeping things in proportion.

It is important to celebrate the occasions when you do Account successfully. According to B.J. Fogg, professor at Stanford University, successfully creating any new habit involves more than just repetition[4]. Rather, the habit is more likely to become fluent if on each occasion you do the habit, in this case Accounting, you generate a positive emotion to go with it. It might sound far-fetched, but as mentioned above, you do, indeed, have the power to create your own emotions, an idea explored by Lisa Feldman-Barrett in *How Emotions Are Made*[5]. Just a metaphorical pat on the back to celebrate each success, may be enough to make the Accounting habit stick. Even if the process of Accounting causes you to notice your habit of beating yourself up when things go wrong, realizing that you engage in this unhelpful pattern is a positive step which you should acknowledge and celebrate.

The problem with Dominating and Marshmallowing, and why Structuring and Nurturing can help

The twin pitfalls that work against developing your personal resilience are the Dominating and Marshmallowing behaviours you use towards yourself (see Figure 5.2). These are common and very human reactions, but in the end, they are self-defeating. Neither the incessant berating of yourself through negative self-talk because you feel overwhelmed by your workload,

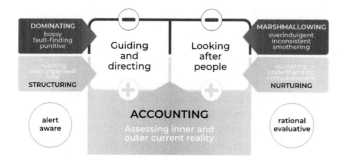

Figure 5.2 Being in Charge behaviours with Accounting.

nor the tendency constantly to focus on what you perceive to be your unique personal flaws, are helpful. Such habits embed within your brain the notion of not being good enough. Equally potent is the adverse impact of Marshmallowing yourself by, for example, 'rewarding' yourself with three bars of chocolate if your boss has criticized you and you are feeling down. This kind of behaviour tends to reinforce the subliminal message of being somehow inadequate.

Dominating pitfalls

If, instead of Accounting, you find yourself being self-critical, or you notice that you are focusing on your mistakes rather than your successes, you may also experience a negative impact on your energy levels. Self-dominating patterns may cause you to give yourself a hard time when you fail to meet a promised target, or on the occasions when you are less than fluent in using the Accounting behaviours you are trying to master. The voice in your head might sound very much like a critical parent, but it will always be rooted in your past, and not relevant to the present moment.

If you constantly punish yourself whenever you feel that you have messed up, the health consequences, in the worst-case scenario, could be severe. Stress triggers are all around you, but if you have made a habit of reacting rather than responding in the face of challenge, then, long-term, you leave yourself open to developing high blood pressure, obesity, type 2 diabetes, cardiovascular disease or Alzheimer's, as well as a host of other diseases detrimental to resilient functioning. Whilst it might be common for leaders or managers to blame themselves for things which are either not their fault or are caused by a combination of people and events, it is not at all helpful to do so. Even if the lion's share of responsibility for something having gone wrong is, in fact, yours to take, it makes much more sense to learn the lessons then move on, than to become caught up in a loop of constant self-criticism.

Marshmallowing pitfalls

When feeling under pressure, you may indulge in Marshmallowing yourself, using self-defeating behaviours which have become familiar to you over time, but which erode your personal resilience. Over-indulgent behaviours, such as excessive drinking or over-eating, for example, may anaesthetize the 'pain' of facing up to a challenge, but the relief is temporary.

Sometimes, it is possible to avoid confronting a problem head-on, and instead to allow the situation to worsen. Members of staff may present as needing a firm guiding hand, but you might use avoidance tactics by Marshmallowing not only yourself, but them too. Your behaviours here may be either over-protective or over-tolerant, but in either case they can have a detrimental effect on the impact you are able to make as a leader, and also, because everything is interconnected, on your life as a whole. In other words, nobody benefits in the end. Many clients who come to coaching fall into this trap, particularly where their desire to please and be liked can lead to them taking on too many of the tasks that should be assigned to others. In spite of knowing this is not the right thing to do, managers who behave in this way end up feeling inadequate, and demoralized.

The value of Structuring and Nurturing yourself

Being productive at work begins with self-care. Firstly, it is important to accept yourself as a human being, and to understand that Nurturing yourself as a leader or manager shouldn't be a bolt-on extra, but rather a central part of how you go about your life and work. Whilst living 'on the edge' may seem attractive, even exciting, if you are not looking after yourself, this will take its toll on your ability to remain resilient. You need to be productive, of course, but if you prioritize this above your wellbeing, you will, at some point, begin to feel the strain. That heady cocktail of adrenalin and cortisol being pumped around your body whenever you react, rather than respond, to those stress triggers, is fine once in a while, but will ultimately drain you of energy, and even worse, could lead to burnout and depression.

As well as adopting self-care habits, it's important to use Structuring behaviours with yourself too. As long as you are maintaining the key resilient principle of remaining flexible, it is good to be firm with yourself, for example. Remaining steady and steadfast on any decisions you have made, whether work-related or personal, is important and will boost your effectiveness, because you won't constantly be caught up in feelings of self-doubt and negative self-talk.

Similarly, assuming your intention is positive, being consistent is important too. Behaviours that are consistent, such as saying what you mean, meaning what you say, and doing it, are important in conveying to others the impression of a congruent leader or manager. But consistency is also important in building your self-efficacy, the belief in your ability to control your behaviours in all situations. Knowing that you can rely on yourself is vital to building resilience. It's important, too, to give yourself a structure in your personal life, as this will directly impact your performance at work. For example, setting boundaries for yourself such as not using the computer within two hours of bedtime, will enable you to sleep more soundly and be more productive as a result.

The case studies below show how using the Functional Fluency Model enabled two managers to work out the reasons for their Dominating and Marshmallowing behaviours. As well as providing them with the opportunity to uncover their unhelpful patterns of behaviour, the model also gave them the information they needed to boost their personal resilience by focusing on some of the key Structuring and Nurturing behaviours.

Case Study: Returning to work

An inexperienced manager had recently returned from maternity leave and was experiencing feelings of inadequacy. Jan felt that she was falling short of what was required at work, and that she would never catch up. To make matters worse, she had begun Dominating herself by engaging in fault-finding and judgmental behaviours, instead of fully taking account of the situation as it was. For example, the IT systems used by her department had changed significantly while she had been on leave, but she was being very critical of herself for not being able to use the new systems, and for having to ask her team how things worked. She was feeling diminished as a person for having to seek support, and seemed completely deflated by the situation, viewing it as a personal fault rather than an inevitable consequence of having had time away.

Jan came to realize that the interpretations she was making of the situation were her own interpretations, and did not necessarily reflect the views of others. She needed to Nurture herself by being compassionate and accepting, and to use Structuring behaviours as well. If she could learn to be more helpful and more compassionate towards herself, whilst showing confidence in her abilities to rebuild her knowledge of the systems, she reasoned that she would reap the benefits of these new behaviours. By reaching out and accepting the assistance of staff rather than being punitive of herself because she needed that help, she could change her deeply rooted patterns of non-resilient reactive behaviours.

As in this case, it can feel 'natural' to engage in negative thinking when under pressure at work. Your thoughts can spiral out of control and leave you feeling incapacitated, and unable to slow down or to take effective action. Because your body believes any message that your brain tells it, this is a major factor in lowering your resilience. To make matters worse, the way you think manifests in your physiology, changing your behaviour as a result. Whilst you may not always be conscious of this behavioural shift, colleagues certainly will be. After all, biologically, they too are hard-wired to be on the lookout for anything that might pose a threat to them.

To reframe the way you see yourself, and therefore the way you present to the world, it helps to begin by talking positively to yourself so that, eventually, this becomes something you do without conscious thought. The key in the first instance is to use the Functional Fluency Model to identify the unhelpful thoughts and emotions you 'indulge' yourself in and to recognize how you need to change these to provide you with energy rather than constantly feeling drained. Once you acknowledge your unhelpful patterns of thinking and behaving, you can use the model to change them. For example, instead of continually telling yourself that you are not an experienced enough manager, you could take a more realistic perspective by acknowledging that there will always be things you don't know, or which are outside your skillset. Instead of Dominating yourself, you could become more compassionate and encouraging with yourself, understanding that you can always learn new skills, and that you always have a choice about how you respond.

Case Study: False Heroism – Saving the Day

During a coaching session, Nita, a department head, wanted to explore the reasons for her procrastination in dealing with particularly important issues that were significant for everyone in the department. She was feeling stressed by what she realized was coming across to others as irresponsibility, especially to those higher up in the organization. In spite of her acute awareness of this unhelpful pattern of behaviour, she felt powerless to change it.

In coaching, Nita used Accounting to consider deeply the reasons for consistently putting off what needed to be done. She ruled out the perhaps more conventional reasons for having adopted this procrastination habit. For example, she wasn't lacking the information she needed in order to take action, nor was she afraid of taking the appropriate steps or of making decisions. However, she realized that the key to her putting things off lay in her tendency to over-indulge her own desire to make work more exciting by leaving things until the last minute.

Whilst Nita was surprised to discover this unhelpful pattern of behaviour, engaging with the Functional Fluency Model illuminated for her the main reason for the choices she was making. In particular, she came to understand that behaving in this way enabled her to become the hero who always saved the day, even if, unhelpfully, others were feeling the pressure of this approach. She acknowledged that whilst this way of working might be fine when working on her own tasks, as head of department it was becoming irresponsible, especially given the negative impact on colleagues. By taking account of the motivations for her behaviour, the situation, and the implications for others, she worked out some new Structuring strategies for changing the way she dealt with these important tasks. For example, she resolved to set firm deadlines for herself and to stick to these, ensuring at the same time that this would help promote the kind of consistency that would benefit others in her department.

In this case procrastination was a form of Marshmallowing, because the Department head was overindulging herself to increase her motivation and personal satisfaction. However, she was behaving irresponsibly, lacking the appreciation or awareness of when enough was enough. Her over-indulgent behaviour of repeatedly ignoring the likely consequences of her actions, was eliciting stress reactions in her body. As indicated above, the frequent production of stress hormones, self-generated as a result of her failure to behave effectively, was likely to have an adverse impact on both her health and on her personal resilience and working relationships with others.

If, like Nita, you have developed a habit of procrastinating at work, it is worth spending time trying to pinpoint your own personal reasons for this. Once you know why you are putting things off, you can decide which functionally fluent behaviours you can use instead. Whilst these behaviours will need practising, in time you should feel less stressed and, happily, more resilient.

Reflection: Affirmations

- Return, in your mind's eye, to the same incident you considered for *Activity 2*. Think about the messages you have since told yourself about the incident, including, if you can, the actual words you have used with yourself when thinking about it. For example, if on one occasion, you failed to meet a deadline, you might have told yourself that you were an 'idiot' for spending too much time responding to emails rather than getting on with the task. Notice the emotional charge around the ways you have been describing this incident to yourself. Take a deep breath, or maybe two, then remind yourself that the incident is now in the past; you cannot change it.
- Pick three or four behaviours from Accounting, Structuring and Nurturing, which, had you used them, both at the time, and since the incident, would have been more effective. For example, if you failed to meet a deadline, using well-organized behaviours and being firm with yourself would probably have worked better. Alternatively, perhaps, you may have shown yourself some compassion by acknowledging that you simply had too much to do. You could then have helped yourself to think through how to deal with the situation. If in the here-and-now, you constantly beat yourself up about what happened, effective Accounting might mean using rational behaviours, where you begin

to think logically, using reason and facts. Decide how you could use these behaviours more in the future.

- Crucially, begin to change the language you use with yourself so that you are more likely to embody the new behaviours in future. If you want to be rational, well-organized and firm, for example, start telling yourself, right now, that this is what you are. Write out three affirmations for each descriptor. It is important that these contain 'I ... ' and are written in the present tense. Here are some examples:

"Before responding, whenever I am faced with a challenge, I think logically, using reason and facts."

"I understand the difficulties I face in reaching the deadline and I can choose to raise the wider problem with others."

"I am very well-organised and do what will make life easier for myself, and all concerned."

- Constantly repeat these affirmations to yourself as you go about your daily life. It may feel unnatural at first, but remember that your mind is always acting on what you tell it. Your habitual way of talking to yourself shapes your behaviours on the outside; you are much more likely to embody the positive behaviours you want if you use positive language with yourself.

How Marshmallowing others can lower your own resilience

Case Study: Feeling the pressure as a Headteacher

Aisha was a primary school headteacher, relatively new to her role, who came to coaching because her job had become all-consuming, and she was struggling to cope. She had little time to spend with her husband and two small children, and her husband was becoming resentful as a result. Although Aisha wanted to sort out these family issues, she seemed to have little time to do so and was always in a rush. Her desire to do a 'good job' meant she frequently stayed behind after work to attend meetings that ran on well into the evening. As a result, she was beginning to feel burned out, had gained weight, and had developed high blood pressure. She urgently needed to do something about it.

Aisha acknowledged that she had set extremely high standards for herself because she was ambitious to move up the career ladder. She had fallen into patterns of Marshmallowing by taking over tasks from others to save time, and to ensure they were completed correctly. One example of this was her management of a staff member who had responsibility for completing an annual report to governors. Aisha felt that the staff member lacked the ability to produce a sufficiently detailed and accurate report, and mistakenly believed that this would reflect badly on her. This had led to Aisha taking over and writing the report herself, and whilst governors were satisfied with it, Aisha frequently felt anxious at having acted in this way.

To make matters worse, Aisha began to realize that this wasn't an isolated incident. In order to expedite procedures within the school, there had been other occasions where she had taken over from staff uninvited, not realizing the long-term hidden harmfulness of this approach. The time taken to complete work that should have been done by others, on top of negotiating the numerous legitimate tasks facing her on a daily basis, meant that she was exhausting herself, and had no time to invest in her own wellbeing.

The agreed solution was to expand her use of Accounting behaviours. In particular, she would become more alert to the impact of her choices on her personal resilience. She resolved to enquire more deeply when confronted with situations where teachers approached her with issues. She reasoned that this would enable her to get a real handle on what exactly would be the best course of action to take if she wanted to develop staff whilst having sufficient energy left over for herself.

This process of slowing down to speed up had a marked impact. Using Accounting to choose which behaviours to blend for maximum effect led to Aisha being able to let go of the need for control. Instead of taking over, she would use Structuring behaviours, remaining firm about her own boundaries and about her expectations of staff. She decided that she would help out when needed by offering guidance, and came to realize that this was a far more empowering approach both for herself and others. She became much better at orchestrating tasks, and at creating boundaries for herself.

A few weeks after learning about Functional Fluency, and implementing changes, she reported thriving in her life at work and home. She had more time to spend with family, and had also begun exercising regularly. As a result, she was happy and confident, the relationship with her husband had improved, and she felt much more able to perform effectively at work.

Developing awareness of your ineffective behaviours is essential in order to change them. Fortunately, the Functional Fluency Model is a useful diagnostic tool for unearthing some of the more deep-rooted reasons for engaging in behaviours that harm your personal resilience. As was the case with this client, it is possible, through Functional Fluency, to gain clarity about the likely impact of your behaviours on others. The increased relational awareness that comes from 'finding yourself' in the model can open up communication channels for more effective communication.

Learning to express yourself by using Spontaneous behaviours

If, at times, you behave in ways that are over-indulgent, and constantly find fault in yourself, or if you are always telling yourself that you are wrong, or denying your own needs and interests, you are not alone. Most of us use unhelpful behaviours from time to time, but our personal resilience becomes eroded if we regularly repeat these ineffective patterns. The emotions prompted by difficult or stressful situations can easily lead to Immature behaviours if your resilience is low.

One of the best ways to promote greater personal resilience in yourself, is to do more of the things that make you unique. This 'essence of you', the creative energy that you have in abundance, but which may need releasing, is well worth discovering. In fact, it is much more accurate to say that connecting with this inner energy involves a process, not of discovery, but of re-discovery, of re-connection. It may very well be buried beneath years of rules by which you have learned to abide, but it is there all right. If for a moment, you doubt the existence of your inner creativity, imagination, and playfulness, consider this: babies do not constantly worry about what people think of them, or about whether they are doing the right thing; they are too busy playing, exploring, and expressing themselves. You were once like that too.

It's important to behave in responsible ways appropriate to your status at work, but it is also important to free yourself up and to bring that childlike quality to your leadership or management style. The case study, below, shows how the client used insights gained from coaching to learn to use Spontaneous Mode behaviours more often (see Figure 5.3).

Case Study 4: The overworked entrepreneur

An entrepreneur came to coaching because she felt overwhelmed, had too much to do, and 'couldn't find the time' to do it. Sarah was director of two businesses, felt stressed out, and was not sleeping well, frequently waking in the night, then getting out of bed to make lists of all the tasks she hadn't yet completed. To make matters worse, she felt she had no time for self-care, or to follow creative pursuits such as the art she loved so much. She was unhappy, and frequently gave herself a hard time by comparing herself to others, for example to those whose businesses she perceived were more successful than her own. Typically, she would find fault in herself, and believed that she 'should' be able to cope. She had fallen into the habit of working constantly, then feeling guilty whenever she took a break.

She discovered that the distinctions between what she said yes to and what she said no to had become blurred. She realized that she had taken on more than most would be able to cope with, that her boundaries were weak, and that she had fallen into a pattern of overestimating her capacity for taking on new work, and other associated activities. For example, as well as her full-time job as a busy entrepreneur, she was a trustee at two charities, where her role involved attending frequent meetings, often in the evenings. She had also set up a small charity of her own, for the benefit of the local community, and for which she worked, unpaid, organizing and attending events, and recruiting and co-ordinating volunteers. She was a trusted business advisor for the local Chamber of Commerce and found it difficult to turn down clients when they were offered to her.

Gradually, Sarah became aware of the negative impact of the choices she was making. She cared passionately for people and for the environment and wanted to do as much as she could to make a positive difference in these areas, but this came at a cost. Whilst clearly compassionate and caring towards others, she found it difficult to show self-compassion, and, through coaching, began to see how Nurturing herself might help. She realized that she had been putting her own needs and interests last.

As a result of these insights, Sarah made some positive changes. She decided to invest more time in self-care, immediately blocking out time for regular outdoor swimming sessions, something she had put off doing for years. She noticed that swimming made her feel young again, and she began to experience the energizing effect of her new hobby. She reported that she felt more alive, as if she were glowing from the inside out, and this was having a positive impact on her energy levels overall.

In a later session, because she now felt much more positive, Sarah was able to focus on how she might use Structuring behaviours with herself, in particular by being firm and consistent about the work she said 'yes' to. This involved Accounting for the fact that she could not take on work and unpaid activities just because they interested her; she needed to *evaluate* the impact of each decision she made. As a consequence, she immediately dropped some of the low value work she was doing that had been adding to her stress levels and lowering her personal resilience.

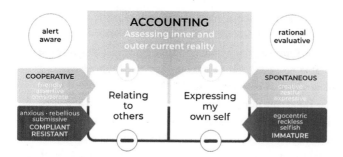

Figure 5.3 Being an Individual behaviours with Accounting.

Reflection: Recapturing your lost spark

- Write a list of all the activities you loved to do as a child – even pillow fighting counts! Spend at least ten minutes on this – more ideas will come if you take a little time over it.
- Tick each of the activities that you still do.
- Draw a circle around the ones you no longer do but would love to take up again.
- Find ways to include these activities in your life. Block out time for them and make your work fit around these, not the other way around.

It's certainly worth unleashing the creative part of your nature as a leader. Whilst it is easy to equate being creative with 'the Arts', the nature of creativity expands way beyond that. Rather, it is about being open to new ideas and ways of doing things, to being playful, to suspending judgement, to being comfortable with uncertainty and in touch with your emotions. Happily, creativity is something you can learn. Try this activity to help release your creativity and boost your personal resilience.

Reflection: Access your creative thinking

- Tune in to where you are or what you are doing when you get your best ideas. This might be when exercising, when out in nature, when you are in a particular place, or when in conversation with a specific person. Build more of this into your life.
- Practise doing little things differently. Take a different route to work, change your morning routine, or hold team meetings in a different location. Be aware of changes to how you feel in these new situations and open up to the possibility of new ideas and insights. Don't forget to write these down!

Using Cooperative behaviours to improve your personal resilience

To be an effective leader it is important to offer warmth by listening with respect. It is vital, too, to consider others' ideas and points of view instead of immediately dismissing them. By doing this, you make team members feel valued and motivated. Whilst all of this seems self-evident, it can be too easy, on a bad day, to fall into behaving reactively. This may mean exhausting yourself by trying to keep everyone happy, but could also entail antagonizing others, either actively or passively, for failing to meet your, perhaps unrealistic, expectations. These are examples of Compliant/ Resistant reactive behaviour.

Showing consideration and being friendly are key Cooperative behaviours likely to benefit everyone. However, just as important is your use of assertiveness. Whilst being open to negotiation, and respecting the views of others is vital, standing up for yourself and putting your own point across, where appropriate, is also important. Being assertive is often confused with aggressive Dominating behaviours such as pointing out faults or using a sarcastic tone with your team, but insights from the following case study demonstrate that this is not what assertiveness really means.

Case Study: When Frustration Takes Over

Michael, who had direct line responsibility for three junior staff members, had been asked to take on additional responsibilities previously done by a different part of his department. Whilst worrying about this, and feeling it wasn't quite fair given the pressure his team was already under, he nevertheless accepted the new tasks. Michael did not talk about the situation with his manager, but instead aired his frustration with team members, and anybody else who would listen. As a result, he was becoming withdrawn at work, would snap at his direct reports, and resented additional requests from his manager. He was beginning to develop a reputation for having a negative attitude, and during a review meeting, his manager suggested personal coaching.

During sessions, Michael came to understand that he often engaged in Compliant / Resistant behaviours with elements of Dominating. Whilst appreciating that he had begun to doubt his own abilities, and that he had a strong perfectionist streak, his key insight from using the Functional Fluency Model was the realization that he was very unassertive. He favoured passive, and sometimes passive-aggressive behaviours, more often than not driven by a fear of conflict, and the need to be liked. Not only this, but he lacked the flexibility to deal effectively with change. He saw things as 'black or white' and struggled with any sense of ambiguity.

By using Accounting to increase his self-awareness, Michael was able to think more rationally. He realized that he had not been taking into account his own needs or those of his direct reports, especially when trying to please his manager by always agreeing to requests. These insights led to him committing to develop his assertiveness skills, to standing up for himself and his team, and to discussing concerns with his line manager before agreeing how to move forward on new tasks. He also recognized that rather than being a sign of weakness as he had previously thought, it was helpful and acceptable to draw on support from the rest of his department.

As well as this, Michael joined a mentoring scheme within the organization, finding it both challenging and stimulating. He met regularly with his mentor and began to keep a journal in which he noted his strengths and achievements. As a result, he started to enjoy work more and found his confidence increased through greater engagement with others. Through this process, he was able to discover how his colleagues handled change and conflict, and this led to him becoming less fearful.

By committing to and maintaining the Accounting habit, Michael became both more adaptable and more flexible at work, key hallmarks of personal resilience. Alongside this, he developed the skills of Cooperative assertiveness, becoming more willing to negotiate and to put his views across in a calm and reasonable manner. This was a big improvement on his former habit of loudly and angrily airing his frustrations to colleagues.

Reflection: Keeping a reflective journal for 30 days

- Over the next 30 days, find time in your day to keep a reflective journal in which you focus on the incidents you encounter at work, and in which you reflect on them.
- Consider the emotions that arose as you dealt with each situation, and where you felt these emotions in your body. Name the emotions. Would you describe them as positive – joy, excitement? Or negative – fear, anger, shame, sadness or disgust? Once identified, avoid attaching too much meaning to your emotions. For example, it is important not to use Dominating behaviours by beating yourself up because you don't think you 'should' feel angry. Emotions are just your body's way of communicating information which you would do well to pay attention to.
- Now write down the behaviours you used in each situation. Use this process to validate and celebrate behaviours that were most likely to benefit everyone and reflect further on behaviours you used that were ineffective.

- Write down what actually happened as a result of your behaviours, then for the ineffective ones, write down alternative functionally fluent behaviours, considering the likely positive impact of using these in similar situations in the future.

Summary

- Leading and managing can be exciting and rewarding, but to be effective at dealing with challenge, it's important to be resilient.
- Resilience is a strength, an attitude and a set of skills which can be learned. Investing in your personal resilience means investing in your wellbeing. Functional Fluency is relevant to your behaviour towards yourself as well as others.
- As a human being, you are hard-wired for survival, but your survival instinct can let you down because usually at work, you're not in real danger. Your body, however, can behave as if it is under attack and this can make you react to problems and issues rather than responding to them. This is usually ineffective.
- Functional Fluency promotes your self-awareness, so you can take control of your responses, and react less often. This will promote both your *intrapersonal* and your *interpersonal* effectiveness and boost your personal resilience.
- Your brain is 'plastic' so you can learn new, more resilient, behaviours. The starting point is Accounting. A key part of Accounting is to pause and to focus on your inner responses to the situations you encounter. You can then choose effective 'external' behaviours likely to benefit everyone.
- Emotions are signals from your body to pay attention to something important. It is important to acknowledge them but not to attach to them.
- For improved resilience, avoid Dominating or Marshmallowing yourself. Aim to Structure or Nurture instead.
- Tapping into Spontaneous mode behaviours and releasing your creativity will make you a more effective leader or manager.
- Cooperative behaviours are also important in your role. It is especially important to be assertive and not to confuse assertiveness with aggression.

Notes

1 Reivich, K. and Shatté, A. (2003) *The Resilience Factor (p.1)*. New York: EPUB.
2 Campbell, J. (2019) *The Resilience Dynamic (p.77)*. Practical Inspiration Publishing.
3 Frankl, V.E. (1946) *Man's Search for Meaning*. Vienna: Verlag für Jugend und Volk.
4 Fogg, B.J. (2020) *Tiny Habits*. London: Virgin Books, Penguin Random House.
5 Feldman-Barrett, L. (2017) *How Emotions Are Made: the secret life of the brain*. London: Pan Macmillan

Chapter 6

Fluent Teamwork

Effective Interaction through Conscious Choices

Hannah Titilayo Seriki

Teams as treasure

The power and value of teams is often underrated. They have always been called upon whenever human beings have thought up and implemented complex new ideas (with the potential to change the world). Neither the pyramids in ancient Egypt, nor the skyscrapers in our modern cities, neither the first animal-drawn cart, nor a high-tech 21st century car, plane or train could ever have come into existence without teams of different subject experts working together to achieve something big. This indicates that a team is not just any old group. It is a very special group of people, who are purposefully drawn together to contribute complementary skills to a common goal, for which they hold themselves mutually accountable. Collective performance is the key factor differentiating a team from any random organizational group. While groups rely on the sum of individual bests for their performance, teams blend together the skills, experiences and insights of several interdependent individuals. In doing so they are able to achieve results that are greater than the sum of their parts.[1]

In the third millennium, a trend among companies around the world has become visible: organizational design is shifting from more traditional hierarchical structures to flatter networks of flexible, interconnected teams. The purpose of this is to tap into the value that teams can contribute to organizations.[2] Teamwork is the interactive process of the team working on its specific task. Research has shown time and again that the quality of this interactive process is a central factor determining the effectiveness of the team.[3] Hey presto! We have found a key to the treasure hidden within your teams, no matter what their task is focussed on

- making decisions (e.g. management teams or teams of experts integrating knowledge, expertise and perspectives to make decisions or solve problems)
- taking action (e.g. production teams or sports teams coordinating and performing physical tasks under time constraints)

DOI: 10.4324/9781003345527-6

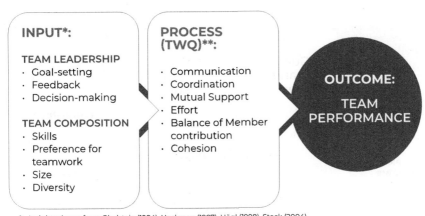

INPUT*:

TEAM LEADERSHIP
· Goal-setting
· Feedback
· Decision-making

TEAM COMPOSITION
· Skills
· Preference for
  teamwork
· Size
· Diversity

PROCESS (TWQ)**:

· Communication
· Coordination
· Mutual Support
· Effort
· Balance of Member
  contribution
· Cohesion

OUTCOME:

TEAM PERFORMANCE

*   Insights drawn from Gladstein (1984). Hackman (1987), Högl (1998), Stock (2004).
** Teamwork quality as defined by Högl and Gemünden (2001)

Figure 6.1 Teamwork as process between input and outcome.

· or innovation (e.g. engineering teams or research groups planning and implementing new concepts, working together in the form of projects with pre-defined time, budget and performance targets)[4]

they simply need to interact together well and they will be successful, enabling the organization to thrive. If only it were that easy! Teamwork is not magic, even if it may look and feel like it when teams get it right. It needs to be consciously enabled and fostered, with awareness for the ingredients conducive to effective interaction.

Since the quest to understand how to access the treasure of teams has been going on at least since the Hawthorne Studies[5] in the 1920s and 30s, we already know a lot about what goes into teamwork. We understand that certain aspects of team leadership and team composition are necessary inputs for the team process to function smoothly. We have also learnt which elements make up high quality teamwork as a process as shown in Figure 6.1.[6]

Fluent teamwork

We can connect the Functional Fluency model with this existing knowledge on teamwork, its antecedents and effects. Seen as a practical menu, enabling team members to choose from a variety of behavioural options, the Functional Fluency model relates directly to those input and process factors required for the team to be effective, i.e. to generate the desired outcomes with the given resources. By using the Functional Fluency model as their

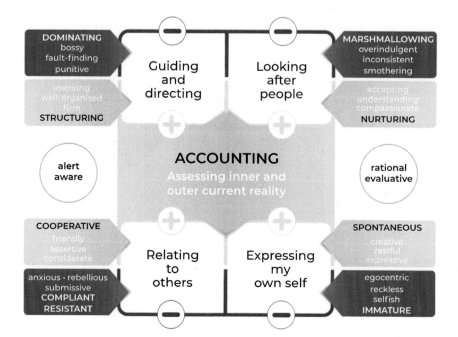

Figure 6.2 The Golden Five and the Purple Pitfalls.

menu, team members learn to choose effective combinations from the behavioural options in any given situation, based on all the information available to them. This is what we call fluent teamwork.

Figure 6.2 is a reminder of the Golden Five and Purple Pitfalls introduced in Chapter 2. Let's have a look at how the Golden Five connect with effective teamwork as described above.

Accounting Mode behaviours ensure that team members *stay present to* (i.e. remain aware of) the inner and outer reality affecting the team. This includes, for example, assessing the skill level present in the team and comparing it with the skills needed for the task at hand. Being alert, aware, rational and evaluative helps team members choose and blend effective mode behaviours well, so that team interaction can be functionally fluent. When teams are learning about Functional Fluency to help them develop effective behaviours for teamwork, it can be useful to do this as a conscious exercise. Once fluent habits have been established in the team, this assessment of reality becomes automatic.

Structuring behaviours are needed for leadership activities, which can be carried out by the team itself as well as by higher-level management. These include being well-organized, firm, and inspiring, which all adds to the effectiveness of setting goals, making decisions and giving feedback.

Sometimes, leaders invest great amounts of energy in these control measures and find, for example, that their team resists the clear decisions they make or the feedback they give. This may be an indication that energy is being used ineffectively and that the leader should look closely at the effective and ineffective sides of control: Structuring vs. Dominating behaviours. Being well-organized also ensures that team members communicate via the most effective channels with just the right frequency ("communication"), that duplication of effort or omission of important tasks is avoided ("co-ordination"), and that team members aim at high performance with evenly distributed workload ("effort").

Nurturing Mode behaviours ensure that team members take care of themselves and each other. They can clearly identify individual and team needs, and recognize the difference between genuine needs and self-indulgent wants. This goes a long way towards maintaining a healthy balance of work and rest, of giving and receiving energy within the team.

For example, if a team is under pressure to complete a great amount of interdependent tasks with a tight deadline and one team member struggles especially to get things done on time, this could lead to any amount of Purple Pitfall behaviour, e.g. blaming the struggling team member for the team's delay, someone else indulgently taking over all that person's tasks, the struggling team member rebelliously deciding they are just not going to do the work, and selfishly taking a couple of extra days off work at the most crucial time. None of this adds to the effectiveness of the team in question.

However, if the other team members can accept that one person is having difficulties, and seek to understand the cause of these, they are able to show compassion towards their teammate and give healthy support, for example by assisting with time-management tools, friendly reminders or answering questions – depending on what is needed. In turn, the struggling teammate accepts that the others need them to deliver and understands that they need to know what is hindering them from completing work on time. This person also needs to be compassionate towards themselves in identifying the cause of difficulties, so as not to waste energy on "self-bashing", but to find the solution needed for the whole team as quickly as possible. Looking back together at goals reached, congratulating and praising each other is also part of Nurturing and very important to keep energy levels up in the team.

Cooperative behaviours are perhaps the most central ingredients to fluent teamwork. The combination of friendliness, assertiveness and consideration makes it possible

- for team members to communicate with each other openly ("communication"),
- for team members to support each other, respect each other and further the development of each others' ideas ("mutual support"),

- for all team members to contribute their knowledge, ideas and experiences in an equal manner ("balance of member contribution"),
- and for team members to appreciate and feel committed to each other ("cohesion").

It is assumed that people who generally prefer working on tasks with others tend to get more readily involved in the interactive team process than those who prefer working on tasks independently. My work with clients as well as personal experience working in teams confirms this. People who have grown up collecting positive experiences interacting with others usually enter into new interactions with more openness and enthusiasm than those for whom interactions with other human beings have been stressful in the past. If a team is made up of people who do not "naturally" prefer working on tasks together, a conscious effort is required to collect new positive experiences during the team's cooperation. With time, this way of interacting becomes increasingly natural, joyful, and a matter of choice for all team members.

Take, for example, Charles, an experienced consultant who has been running his own consultancy for many years. When Charles joins a new consulting firm as a partner, he finds it difficult to bring his own ideas in when the other partners are contributing such different points of view and ways of doing things with passion and enthusiasm. Sometimes Charles decides to just be quiet and keep his own ideas to himself so as not to be seen as the spoil-sport by the others (Compliant). At other times he bursts out that he does not agree with any of the ideas that have been discussed and refuses to support them (Resistant). He could even go so far as to demand that everyone needs to change their way of working to suit what he is used to, threatening to leave this consultancy otherwise, and to go back to running his own in competition with the new partnership (Immature). In reaction to this, the other partners could all gang up against Charles, fight him out of the firm and continue to compete with him for business.

Alternatively, the entire team of partners could take a step back, look at each other with friendliness (remembering what they appreciated about each other and what made them want to work together in the first place), take time to truly listen to each others' views and ideas (presented assertively and with conviction), and carefully consider each of them. The team members may find that newly absorbed information brings to light new possibilities that were not considered before. These may require everyone to adapt some of their previous ideas on route to new, innovative solutions.

Spontaneous behaviours inject energy, life, enthusiasm, and creativity into the team process. If each team member gets and takes the opportunity to express themselves freely, following their own interests and impulses imaginatively, playfully and bravely, truly new ideas can and will emerge and be developed. Of course, this expression of self needs to remain appropriate to the team members' age and context, so that cooperation continues and Purple Pitfalls, such as the ones described in the example above, are avoided.

The Golden team (example)

Imagine a cross-functional team working together to develop a new strategic plan for their organization to deal with the challenges of a volatile, uncertain, complex world, and increasing competitiveness in their market. Creativity and innovation are among the organization's core values, thus brilliant new ideas and solutions are expected from the team. New business areas are to be identified, and customer relationships strengthened, leading to increased turnover, profit and organizational growth.

The team consists of five members, who work together part time, enthusiastically contributing many separate new ideas. Team members enjoy being able to do their own thing, and can become quite attached to their own ideas. Learning from the Functional Fluency model, they allow themselves the joy of expressing their ideas, while noticing when individual attachments to certain ideas or ways of doing things may endanger progress for the team as a whole. They alternate times of individual creative development with co-operative sessions involving the whole team. When discussions during these sessions become heated, team members remind themselves that assertively pitching their own idea to the others can and must go hand in hand with truly considering the ideas of others. Only if they succeed in doing both, can completely new implementable solutions emerge. When this happens, what a joy it is for everyone involved, and the team can celebrate its successes along the way. Team members who tend to become anxious or upset recognize when their own behaviour becomes ineffective. They are then able to pause before reacting even more. They can identify what triggered them into behaving ineffectively and choose a more effective alternative going forwards.

Regular Accounting ensures that team decisions are taken based on what is really going on at present within the environment, and within the team. "Do I and others benefit?" becomes a team mantra – the question that team members always come back to. The word "benefit" is used here in the sense of leading towards the team goal, as well as fulfilling individual needs. These status quo checks also enable the team to recognize when Structuring or Nurturing behaviour is needed, e.g. clear guidelines, information and goals, or understanding and kindness towards each other. These are all elements of the team's interactive process, which are strongly influenced not just by the team leader. All members of the team play a part in ensuring that the team's needs are fulfilled. By focussing on the Golden Five, this team succeeds not only in developing a new strategic plan within the agreed timeframe, but also in communicating this plan within the organization in such a way that those involved in implementing the new plan are inspired and equipped to do so effectively.

Reflection

Even if you may be thinking at this point that this "golden team" sounds too good to be true, take some time to connect to the story above. Perhaps read it through again, slowly.

Do parts of this story remind you of similar experiences you have had working within a team? Focus on your positive team experiences, however big or small they may be.

- In those moments when working interactively with others went well for you, which of the effective behavioural modes (Structuring, Nurturing, Accounting, Cooperative, Spontaneous) were you using?
- What helped you develop this behaviour (e.g. specific incidents, conversations, lived examples, input from others)?
- How do you want to build on this as you work with teams currently and in the future?

Fluent leadership in teams

As mentioned earlier, leadership activities such as goal-setting, feedback, and decision-making are vital for teamwork be successful. Some teams officially allocate the role of Team Leader to one person – others practise shared leadership, deliberately deciding against hierarchy within the team, and emphasizing collaborative decision-making and shared responsibility for outcomes. The team leader is ideally a person with experience and strengths, using Accounting behaviours. This means they are alert, aware, rational and evaluative. Whether the team is assigned a team leader or not, leadership in a fluent team is always partly the responsibility of all. Because teamwork is about bringing different skills and abilities together, each member of the team will have specific areas of expertise , in which they need to take the lead. Even if you are not "the team leader" there will be aspects of the team's work where you can contribute by, for example, summarizing developments, inspiring others, motivating colleagues, appreciating them, resolving difficulties and sharing perceptions. All this is part of leadership.

Whoever takes leadership responsibility has to be familiar with the intricacies of "Being in Charge". Being in Charge of a team is not just defined by what you do as a team leader (leadership activities), but – possibly even more importantly – by who you are. The team leader is a living, breathing example demonstrating to the other team members how to authentically show up as a human being. To be able to do this, you need to know yourself pretty well, to be able to work with your strengths, and your weaknesses. Before you can lead others, you have to gather some positive experience leading yourself. Your personal way of leading the team springs from your own internal attitude towards yourself and others.

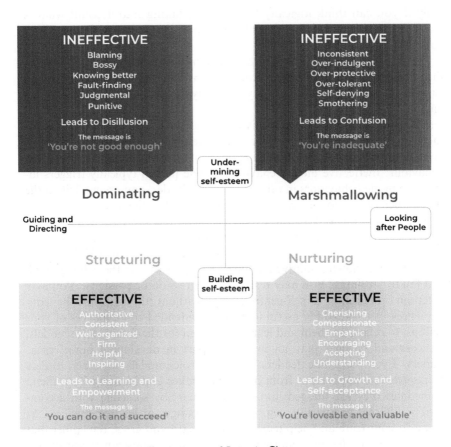

Figure 6.3 Effective and ineffective ways of Being in Charge.

Figure 6.3 reminds us of the effective ways in which we can Be in Charge as well as the ineffective behaviours we are sometimes triggered into using as leaders. The messages at the bottom of the purple and golden fields are often unconsciously held beliefs, which are implicitly communicated to others through our behaviour. In our interaction with the team it is important that we focus on the Golden Five, through which we can empower others, and steer clear of the disempowering Purple Pitfalls. Sometimes, leaders who want to work on increasing their effectiveness with the Functional Fluency model, focus on what the model indicates they are "supposed" to do. It is often more helpful to begin by honestly examining our own beliefs about the people we are leading and understanding where these beliefs come from. Then we can also truly grasp whether these beliefs are valid and beneficial to the team leader as well as the team in the current situation. The behavioural choices you make must make sense to you.

Only if you can think logically for yourself, taking into account what is really going on right here, right now (Accounting), can you fluently lead your team.

The internal attitude from which we communicate with others influences the underlying current of this communication. Thus, a team leader who feels superior to the team members may try really hard to build Structuring behaviour, e.g. by setting goals and timelines for the team. Due to their internal attitude, the way they do this will still come across as Dominating for those on the receiving end. They are therefore likely to unconsciously follow an invitation to react with, for example, Compliant/Resistant or Immature behaviour. Ineffective mode behaviour by one person typically triggers ineffective mode behaviours in others, too. As a leader, you are modelling the type of behaviour you expect to see in others within the team.

As a human being, you will experience "bad days" where, under stress, mindfulness may disappear out of the window, and ineffective autopilot reactions kick in. Perhaps you focus on what has gone wrong (fault-finding) and put people down (punitive/blaming). You may overdo the helping hand, and fail to set limits. You may resist with aggression or passivity. You may react on impulse in a self-centred way, without thought for the consequences. It is incredibly useful to notice unintended consequences of your actions, to reflect on them and learn from them for the future. Role models, mentors and coaches play an important part in developing ourselves as leaders. Even long-time leaders, who are role models to other leaders themselves are not exempt from making mistakes and learning from them. Sometimes they are nudged into this awareness by someone with a completely different perspective, e.g. someone younger or less experienced. As you lead your team and help team members learn and grow, remember that you too are on a learning journey and your interaction with the team will inevitably present you with learning opportunities, too.

One big learning area for many leaders is managing performance. Here again, it is useful to understand how we have experienced our own performance being managed in the past – by other authority figures, and by ourselves. In order to manage performance effectively we need to recognize what has been done well, and what needs improvement. Evaluative judgement of behaviour and outcomes is needed here (not fault-finding). Effective performance management includes the "You can do it" and "You are ok as you are" beliefs, two-way communication and mutual agreement on the performance goals. For a more in-depth exploration of performance management, see Chapter 3.

Even if your role is officially team leader, you are also a member of the team, who, in addition to needing to be good at Being in Charge (i.e. Guiding and Directing and Looking after People), also sets the tone for how Cooperation and Spontaneity are lived in the team. Collaborating with others, inviting feedback, and respecting other people's contributions and points of view will add to your effectiveness as a team leader. Again you are modelling the type of behaviour you expect and need from your team. Should you ever be unable to work for a while, your team will continue to work towards the common goal – emulating what they have learnt from you. A too strongly pronounced hierarchy easily becomes detrimental to cooperation and creativity and may also stand in the way of the team's trust-building process. As I explain later in the section on diversity, members of a fluent team work through their own vulnerabilities, and do not use the vulnerabilities of others against them. This, of course, includes the team leader, who can support trust-building within the team by encouraging team members to see their colleagues as human. One way to do this is to provide situations that facilitate the safe sharing of personal stories. What better way to begin this as a team leader than by sensitively sharing some personal stories of your own? (Spontaneous)

The leader as part of a human system

By now you will have noticed that we recognize the team leader as a vital part of the team system, connected to and influencing the other team members through thoughts, feelings and actions. Your emotions as a team leader play a bigger role here than many are aware of. Because emotions are contagious,[7] you are shaping team culture or the team's "vibe" with your feelings. The hidden emotions of one person can affect another, like a contagious disease. As a leader you can practice picking up on this. You can use your ability to sense and transmit emotions consciously. Becoming aware of the emotions of others in the team can assist you in recognizing the individual needs of team members. You can cater to those needs, and thus enable people to grow. You can also focus on your own positive emotions, express them, and transmit them to the team. If this idea seems strange to you, try exploring it for a while on your own or with the support of a coach.

Throughout the team's journey, navigating challenges and triumphs in the different stages of the team's development, effective leaders remain focussed on a clear purpose, which they share with their team. Be careful not to get distracted along the way by short-term successes or the allure of power. Remember that not your own heroic image, but what you accomplish through and with your team is the key to long term success.

Reflection

I invite you to reflect for yourself on the topics discussed above. The following questions may support your reflections:

• What is your goal with the team your are currently leading?
• (Is there a public and private version? If yes, can they be integrated?)

- What is your greatest strength as a leader?
- (Is there an effective and ineffective side to that?)

When teamwork is tricky

Earlier in this chapter, we looked at a team that had mastered fluent team-work, interacting with behaviours from the Golden Five for the benefit of all. Of course life, especially life in teams, does not just consist of golden moments. Functional Fluency also describes the ineffective behaviours. Old habits can trip you up, and you react rather than respond. Should this happen as you are interacting with others in a team, your automatic, emotionally charged, re-actions will trigger automatic reactions in other team members, too. Unless someone remembers to go back to those Accounting behaviours to work out what is actually going on, and what is needed to get back onto the "golden track", an awful lot of the energy available in the team will be used up in tedious, nerve-wrecking ineffective behaviours and processes. The previous section showed that leadership can make all the difference.

Case Study

The "golden" team described earlier may not have started their work together with the approach they later learnt to grow into. Now imagine a different team, also made up of five members, also tasked to create a new strategic plan for their organization. The five members are all under immense pressure to prove their worth in the organization. They are all the heads of their own departments, and most of them are more comfortable heading up their own team than working together in a team of peers. Working together with other department heads seems like an uncomfortable new requirement that the CEO has conjured up. They are sitting around a table in their first team meeting to kick-off the strategy project.

Daniel has brought along a presentation with his already well-developed ideas for a new strategy. Dominique feels challenged by this. She throws in a few ideas of her own and points out why Daniel's ideas will not work. Rona becomes anxious about being dominated by the older Daniel and Dominique. As a young, female leader in her own right, she feels that she needs to put her foot down from the start to show the others that she will not be pushed around. With a loud voice and arms crossed over her chest she states that the ideas of Daniel and Dominique are equally boring and old-fashioned, not at all what is needed in this day and age. You can feel the temperature as well as tempers in the room begin to rise. Mary very softly and sweetly insists that everyone has contributed really good points. She offers to write up all the ideas contributed, and start forming them into an integrated proposal for a new strategy. "Great, I want to get out of here anyway," says Ivan, getting up and walking towards the door. He really does not feel like being in a room with these people any longer. Christopher is finding it hard to breathe. As the newest member of this team of organizational leaders, he feels both intimidated and frustrated by what he is witnessing. He was looking forward to getting to know the others a bit better, and having a chance to contribute some thoughts he had been playing around with. Instead, he has spent the past half hour nodding to views he does not really agree with, and not saying a word. Now it looks as if the meeting is coming to a close and he definitely does not want to rock the boat. "Right," says Daniel. "Looks like that's it for today. I'll let the boss know we're making progress. See you next week. I'll have my secretary send out a calendar entry."

This team has got off to a tricky start to say the least. Can you recognize what kinds of behaviour the first letters in the team members' names stand for?

Here they are in order of appearance:

- Daniel and Dominique both represent Dominating. Do you recognize their behaviour as blaming, bossy, knowing-better, fault-finding, judgemental or punitive?
- Rona represents the Resistant part of Compliant/Resistant. Do you see that she is anxious, defiant and/or rebellious?
- Mary represents Marshmallowing. In this little story, you can observe her behaving in these ways: smothering, over-protective, self-denying.
- Ivan represents Immature. Have a look at how he displays egocentric, inconsiderate, childish or selfish behaviour.
- Christopher represents the Compliant part of Compliant/Resistant. Do you see that he acts inhibited, and anxious?

I invite you to stay with the impressions from this little story for a bit, and reflect on the following questions:

- What came up for you as you read the description of this team experiencing its first team meeting (feelings, body sensations, images, thoughts, memories)?
- What made it so easy for everyone to start off with ineffective behaviour?
- What do you think this team needs in order to have a chance of success going forward?

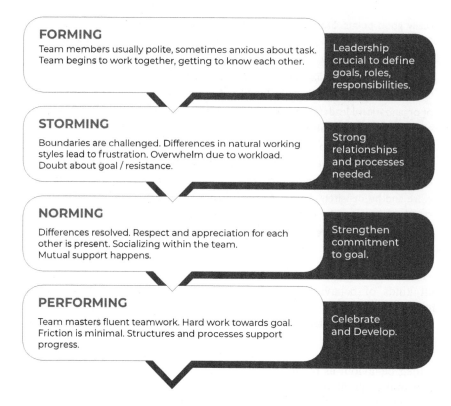

FORMING
Team members usually polite, sometimes anxious about task. Team begins to work together, getting to know each other.

Leadership crucial to define goals, roles, responsibilities.

STORMING
Boundaries are challenged. Differences in natural working styles lead to frustration. Overwhelm due to workload. Doubt about goal / resistance.

Strong relationships and processes needed.

NORMING
Differences resolved. Respect and appreciation for each other is present. Socializing within the team. Mutual support happens.

Strengthen commitment to goal.

PERFORMING
Team masters fluent teamwork. Hard work towards goal. Friction is minimal. Structures and processes support progress.

Celebrate and Develop.

Figure 6.4 Four stages of team development (adapted) as identified by Tuckman.[8]

The four stages of a team's development, as shown in Figure 6.4, come in handy here. They help us gain clarity on what may lie behind the trickiness of teamwork in each stage, and what kind of behaviour is needed most at this point, especially from a leadership perspective.

Forming

The main questions at the beginning of a team's process are all about assessing reality and growing team-awareness (Accounting):

- What is our task?
- Why did we get that task?
- Who are we?
- What are our resources?
- How do we work together?

Typically, at the beginning of a project, few commonalities exist among team members apart from their common task. Over time and managed well, these teams have the chance to build a strong emergent culture as shared member expectations facilitate communication and performance.[9]

Even though shared leadership is an important part of teamwork, at this stage of the team process, a team benefits from an experienced person to guide and direct the disparate individuals into forming a cohesive team. All this points towards the role of team leader. In the example of the "tricky team", the direction for the team was not clear, and nobody at that first meeting was alert or aware enough to bring the team's attention to this. Allan (the CEO of the company, referred to at the end of our story so far as "the boss") is needed at the table, representing Accounting Mode with alert, aware, evaluative, grounded, enquiring and rational behaviour. This would help the team to start effectively by having a look together at the team's task, its meaning and impact for each team member, their department, the entire organization, and its stakeholders. The team members also need time and space to get to know each other and the team leader can facilitate this.

Storming

The team in our example unconsciously tried to skip the forming stage, and jumped right into storming, the stage in which boundaries are challenged, differences in personal working styles become evident and team members feel frustrated, overwhelmed and/or resistant. This is not at all unusual, so beware! The "tricky team example" should clarify how important the forming stage is as a basis for "productive" storming to happen in the next step.

We can assume that in our "tricky team", lack of leadership, and high levels of anxiety triggered the team members into ineffective behaviour. This looked different for the various team members, as each one reacted by going to their default automatic behaviour, developed since childhood, based on what once helped them survive or get acknowledgement in difficult situations. None of them seemed able to tap into and use Accounting behaviours, which are needed to respond consciously to what is going on in the here and now. Perhaps Daniel protected himself from discomfort with the uncertain task by preparing a presentation. This created the illusion for him of being on top of things. Growing up, Daniel's parents had always expected him to be the perfect example for his smaller siblings to look up to. Appearing to know everything had helped him then. He had never thought about this deeply entrenched behavioural pattern, how it served him, and where its limits were. So, it remained an automatic reaction, just like Dominique's desire to challenge, Rona's demonstrative rebelling, Mary's attempts at doing everything for everyone, so that the others may feel better, etc.

In this stage it is also important for each team member to take into account their own personal goals as well as hidden factors such as fears, concerns, and intentions. For example, Mary is driven by the fear of not being liked. Dominique's intention is for Daniel not to succeed, as they are competitors for the next possible promotion level in the organization. These are not issues that can be addressed in the team at the beginning, as trust has not yet been built by the individuals. On the individual level however, awareness of "what else" is going on under the surface helps to recognize when energy, for example to defend a certain idea, is put to good use and when it would be wasted, as the real issue is something completely different.

This is the stage in which uncomfortable emotions show up most strongly, making it difficult for team members to Account - stay alert, aware, rational, and evaluative. The team leader can help the team members develop the necessary awareness by using a coaching style of leadership: asking questions and creating opportunities for the team to reflect on these (individually and together). The team benefits from discussing what is hindering them from reaching their goals, and what can help them become more effective as a team. The Functional Fluency model can be used as a very practical menu of behaviour at this stage of a team's life. As the team recognizes which behaviours are currently present, and which are needed in the different roles, they can establish processes that benefit the team in working towards their goal, and strengthen relationships between team members.

Norming

Once the team has managed to get through the storming phase, working together begins to feel more comfortable. Team members have learnt to resolve differences with each other. They have got to know and appreciate the strengths of their teammates, as well as the areas in which each one needs support. This is a time to really practise Cooperative and Spontaneous ways of behaving. They are able to ask each other for help as well as to provide constructive feedback to colleagues within the team. The team has developed into a cohesive unit, even socializing together with increasing ease. This is also a time to beware of becoming complacent. Does the team still have the agreed goal in mind? How has commitment towards this overarching goal developed? It may need strengthening.

In the norming phase, the team leader can best support the team by keeping the goal in mind, tracking the team's progress, and alerting the team when their actions are leading them off course. At this point, the team leader can steer from within the team, using Cooperative behaviours. It can be a very positive experience to lead a team of empowered individuals with assertive friendliness, consideration, and adaptability. This allows the team as a whole to remain creative and full of energy.

Perhaps this is also a point in the team's process, where input from or cooperation with other teams within the organization is needed. On top of fluent teamwork within the team, which is being developed well, inter-team cooperation can become a decisive factor on route to the big goal. What team members have been practising internally, the team as a unit can now replicate in their interaction with other units within the organizational network.

Performing

In the performing stage, the team masters fluent teamwork. Team members work hard, focusing on reaching their goal, with hardly any friction at all. The structures and processes to support this are in place. Team members enjoy taking part in creating something new and valuable. When things are going well and teams are intensely focused on the end goal, they sometimes forget to celebrate all the milestones they are reaching on their way. Celebrating successes is, however, important for the team. It gives the team members time to pause, reflect, stay connected to one another, acknowledge what they have done well, so that they can continue to build on this as they move ahead in their work together. The team leader does well to encourage Spontaneous behaviours here. For example, a celebratory lunch may be held at the end of each week, at which the team members are asked to express what went really well this week, and congratulate themselves for that. Team members can thank each other for specific things they did that really helped along the way. This way the team remains infused with positive energy, and avoids teamwork becoming mechanistic.

Another point the team leader can concentrate on in this phase is identifying what each team member needs to further develop, and unfold their full potential. Each team member has probably found their niche in the team by now, and is doing what they do best. Dependencies on individuals may be developing. These could become pitfalls if the specialist team members become unavailable for any reason. Consequently, learning from each other, and building some extra skills, ideally continues. Using Accounting and Nurturing behaviours, the team leader recognizes when the team members are becoming too separated into their specialist areas and, while cherishing their expertise, encourages them to share their tasks and skills with others (e.g. in a buddy system). This way, team members learn to appreciate even more what the others are doing, and develop additional skills themselves at the same time. The team avoids teamwork suddenly becoming tricky again.

Reflection

I invite you again to take some moments to reflect on the developmental process of teams described here and on your role as a leader during these stages:

If you are working with a team right now, which stage would you say you are in?

- What are typical triggers into ineffective behaviour for your team?
- Which effective behaviours are being used?
- Which immediate next step is necessary for your team to move through the current stage into the next one?

Diversity in teams – trick or treat?

As mentioned earlier in this chapter, the ingredients combined in composing/creating a team influence the team's process. Diversity within the team plays an important role here, and thus deserves a closer look.

"Diversity" refers to differences among people that affect their interactions and relationships. These differences can be factual, or perceived to exist by members of the team. Differences in observable attributes such as age, gender, race, ethnic background as well as differences in less visible or underlying attributes, like level and style of education, technical abilities, functional background, organisational tenure or personality are all part of what we call "Diversity". All those factors that may define our identity can also differentiate us from other people. We have observed that if team members have a mindset of diversity, fluent teamwork as we understand it is enabled. At the core of this mindset of diversity lies an understanding of who I am, and an openness to the perceptions of others. It is clearly rooted in Accounting behaviour.

A dominating view in the literature on teamwork was for a long time that diversity in its different forms has negative effects on the team process, such as severe communication problems and conflicts. Diverse teams are particularly vulnerable to interaction problems that may affect team cohesion. Members of diverse teams see and interpret their environment in completely different ways. Different ways of behaving and communicating are "normal" for them. Team members often find themselves more attracted to people who they perceive to be more similar to themselves than to people who are "different". We tend to stick to what we know and to mistrust those who we believe are unlike us. This mistrust stems less from actual dislike of the person (who we do not know), and more from an inability to accurately interpret the way they look, speak or behave. So, working in diverse teams can be incredibly tricky.

However, research also shows that for the accomplishment of creative and innovative tasks, a team may do better with multiple experiences and perspectives.[10] Although they encounter more process problems than homogeneous teams, diverse teams also have the potential to achieve higher productivity and creativity. They are never in the middle – they either do really badly or really well. Due to the varied backgrounds, they can create more ideas, alternatives, and problem solving solutions. They are more motivated to realistically consider alternative courses of action (less Groupthink). In sum, for diverse teams and their leaders, balancing creativity and cohesion (unity) is particularly challenging. It takes plenty of awareness and practice to get this right. What a treat it is to observe diverse teams that do manage to develop fluent teamwork and excel.

On our mission to drive and strengthen fluent teamwork, we advocate the synergistic approach to diversity, which includes an awareness of both the difficulties and potential advantages of diversity. We acknowledge that our ways may differ and that none is inherently superior to the other. Nurturing behaviour, especially accepting people for who they are and valuing them as such, helps us in the practice of this approach. The beauty of synergy is that differences are resolved, as the strengths of each position are maximized, and the weaknesses minimized. After all, teamwork as we describe it here is based on a need for different people with different, complementary, skills, experiences and approaches.

Imagine you have a person with a simple task. The person is really good at doing this task. Then this task needs to be done many times – more times than one person can manage. In this case, carbon copies of the one person would be a good solution. If the task is complex and needs different skills and personalities, then carbon copies are not a solution. You will rather be glad to have diversity – and true teamwork.

My reflections and observations, as I have worked with diverse teams in various organizations over the past decade, lead me to the conclusion that successful diversity management interventions have Accounting behaviours at their core – a realistic assessment of what is really present and needs attention within the team and its context. The forming and storming stages may require extra time and energy for a more diverse team. The behaviours and actions needed remain the same as described previously. In the case of diverse teams it is especially important to acknowledge differences and identify commonalities, of which there may be many more that the team members initially assume.

For example, one team member may naturally emphasize structure very strongly. This person is forever making plans and tracking progress. Another team member is inclined to work in a very Spontaneous way, following sudden impulses or urges. These two can drive each other up the wall, if each one focuses on defending their own way of working. With a common goal in mind, and looking at the Functional Fluency "map", they can see the "gold" in what each one is contributing. The Spontaneous team member avoids going off on a tangent on her own and thanks the Structured team member for keeping her on track. The Structured team member avoids getting stuck in the planning and measuring, and truly appreciates the Spontaneous team member for getting them into action, shining the light on new, creative possibilities. This is only possible if the different team members are able to use Cooperative behaviours, which includes friendliness and consideration towards each other. That can be quite a challenge. In a fluent team, each member contributes their own flavour and the team needs it all.

The commonalities, as well as the different strengths and skills that team members bring to the team, enable a culture of belonging to develop. It may be useful for the team to discuss together what it means for each person to truly belong, and what is therefore needed in the team for each person to feel they truly belong in this team.

Diversity and vulnerability

This is a good basis for the team's storming processes to happen. An extra dose of Cooperative behaviour is needed to tackle difficulties with difference openly and honestly. As we have seen in the previous section, this is especially difficult when people are feeling anxious or vulnerable. The more diverse a team is, the more vulnerable people will probably feel with each other. It takes courage to face up to your own vulnerability (instead of hiding it from yourself and others), and to take a chance on these strange people you need to work with. As Linda Kohanov[11], a world-renowned author, leadership coach and horse-trainer, so aptly puts it: "As we gain confidence in taking chances, we recognize vulnerability as a friend. It encourages us to rise above old patterns, teaching us to adjust fluidly not only to what is, but also to what can be, allowing us to dance with the constantly shifting currents of a life lived artfully, consciously – and ultimately, joyfully. Because when vulnerability is no longer seen as the enemy, we can embrace it for what it truly is: the gateway to freedom and self-mastery." This is very closely aligned with the intention behind Functional Fluency: to support people in learning to react less (automatically) and respond more, consciously choosing from available options, so that they may thrive at life.

For members of diverse teams this presents an unexpected gift. Navigating their way through the tricky team process they are repeatedly confronted by their own vulnerabilities, triggering them to react with ineffective behaviour. Using Accounting behaviours helps to stay present to what is happening. Using Nurturing behaviours, especially acceptance towards self and others, helps people work with their own vulnerability and allow others to work through theirs. Engaging with vulnerability in a curious, playful way can enable people to express themselves freely within the team. No wonder Brené Brown[12], researcher, author and expert on vulnerability calls vulnerability the birthplace of creativity and innovation. If the members of our diverse team have come this far in their tricky process, and can now consciously choose responses, they will not just be enabling the team to succeed in reaching its goal. They will also be taking giant steps in developing themselves in Functional Fluency – the art and skill of interpersonal effectiveness.

So, if you are working with a diverse team right now, we invite you to see the difficulties as well as the gifts that this opportunity presents you with.

Reflection

When you are ready, take some time to reflect on the following questions:

- What do you find difficult as you work with difference?
- In which situations do you feel vulnerable?
- How can you respond effectively to vulnerability?

Summary

In summary, the following points characterize the functionally fluent team:

- Fluent teams blend together the skills, experiences and insights of several interdependent individuals, and in doing so are able to achieve results that are greater than the sum of their parts.
- The team members learn to choose effective combinations from the behavioural options the Functional Fluency model offers based on all the information available to them.
- The team leader is especially strong in Accounting, continuously develops themselves, and believes in people's ability to develop and succeed.
- The team leader is equally skilled at Being in Charge and Being an Individual behaviours, and thus leads with authority and authenticity.
- The team invests time and energy into getting to know each other (with strengths and weaknesses), and agreeing on tasks and goals at the beginning of their process together.
- They accept the challenges that come with different viewpoints and ways of doing things, allow themselves and others to fall into Purple Pitfalls at times (to be human), and support each other in developing effective ways of working together using the Golden Five.
- Members of a fluent team work through their vulnerabilities and do not use the vulnerabilities of others against them.
- They have fun, celebrate their successes, and while they can reflect deeply and work hard, they do not take themselves too seriously.
- Fluent teams are the ones that all others in the organization want to work with, too.

Notes

1 For some research on this see for example Katzenbach, J.R. and Smith, D.K. (1993) *The Wisdom of Teams – Creating the High-Performance Organization.* Boston: Harvard Business School Press and Cohen, S. G., and Bailey, D.E. (1997) "What Makes Teams Work: Group Effectiveness Research from the Top Floor to the Executive Suite", in: *Journal of Management, 23 (3), 239–290.*

2 See Deloitte *Global Human Capital Trends* (2016) https://www2.deloitte.com/za/en/pages/human-capital/articles/2020-human-capital-trends. html

3 See, for example, Högl, M. and Gemünden, H.G. (2001) "Teamwork Quality and the Success of Innovative Projects – a theoretical concept and empirical evidence", in *Organization Science, 12 (4), 435–449.*

4 For different types of teams and their levels of interdependence see, for example, Mankin, D. et al. (1996) Teams and Technology – fulfilling the promise of the new organization, Boston, MA: Harvard Business School Press; Högl, M. (1998) *"Teamarbeit in Innovativen Projekten – Einflussgrossen und Wirkungen".* Wiesbaden; Gabler Verlag; DeChurch, L.A. and Mesmer-Magnus, J.R. (2010) "The Cognitive Underpinnings of Effective Teamwork: a meta-analysis", in *Journal of Applied Psychology, 95 (1), 32–53.*

5 The Hawthorne Studies conducted by Harvard Business School researchers Elton Mayo and Fritz Roethlisberger highlighted the positive effects of teamwork and social interaction in an organizational setting.

6 In 2001, management scholars Martin Högl and Hans-Georg Gemünden defined and validated six facets of "Teamwork Quality" as a measure for the team's interactive process. See note 3 above.

7 See work by anthropologist E. Richard Sorensen on "Sociosensual Awareness" and psychiatrist Elio Frattaroli on "Affect Contagion" in Frattaroli, E. (2001) *Healing the Soul in the Age of the Brain – becoming conscious in an unconscious world,* New York, Viking.

8 Tuckman, B.W. (1965) "Developmental Sequence in Small Groups", in *Psychological Bulletin, Vol. 63, June 1965.*

9 This is one of the findings of Early, P.C. and Mosakowski, P.M. (2000) "Creating hybrid team cultures: an empirical test of transnational team functioning", in *Academy of Management Journal, 43(1), 26–49.*

10 See for example Gladstein, D.L. (1984) "Groups in context – a model of task group effectiveness", in *Administrative Science Quarterly, 29, 499–517;* Adler, N.J. (2002) *International Dimensions of Organizational Behaviour,* 4th edition. Cincinnati, Ohio: South-Western College Publishing.

11 Kohanov, L. (2013) *The Power of the Herd – a non-predatory approach to social intelligence, leadership and innovation.* Novato: New World Library.

12 Brown, Brené, (2013) *The Power of Vulnerability: Teachings of Authenticity, Connection and Courage.* Audiobook, Sounds True Inc.

Chapter 7

Embracing Challenging Relationships for Effective Leadership

Three perspectives

Leona Bishop and Martin van den Blink

Introduction

One of the key complaints and/or concerns in corporate life is interpersonal relationship challenges. Interpersonal relationships can be tough. If only everyone saw it your way! The reality is that conflicts, misunderstandings and friction in organizations often originate in the expectation that other people have the same motivation, drives, values and views as ourselves. In most organizations this is not the case, however.

When people work together, it's unlikely that they will always get along. However, breakdowns in communications in the workplace due to poor interpersonal relationships, can knock things off track, and prevent the organization from reaching its full potential. It can lead to frustration, loss of productivity, missed deadlines, lack of engagement and energy within the workplace, and in the worst case, illness, dismissals, or tedious and nasty court cases. Energy spent on tensions and relationship difficulties in the workplace cannot be spent on positive outcomes for the organization and its people and clients, so you need to develop a healthy environment in which to work, and find ways to resolve issues.

The central question in this chapter is how to embrace challenging relationships in the workplace in order to create a positive, trusting, inclusive organizational culture. Previous chapters have explored the value of Functional Fluency in management and leadership relationships inside ourselves, with other individuals at different levels in an organization, and in teams. In this chapter we will explore an extended case study which considers the individual and group perspective, and also shows how the organizational system influences the ability of leaders and their teams to achieve their goals through healthy flourishing relationships. It shows how not only interpersonal relationships but also the culture of an organization can benefit from being viewed through the lens of Functional Fluency.

If you haven't yet read any other chapter, our advice is to read at least chapters 1 to 4 first. Before plunging into the case (the Story of Delivery), we will briefly touch on the added value of Functional Fluency when dealing

DOI: 10.4324/9781003345527-7

with interpersonal challenges. We will then walk you through the case step by step by viewing it through the lens of Functional Fluency from the three perspectives: individual, group and organization. Throughout the chapter we will give you some relevant theory, and show you what you can gain from actively applying Functional Fluency in your organization. Each section on a perspective ends with a reflection exercise.

Added value of Functional Fluency

You may already know that interpersonal difficulties can occur for numerous reasons such as difference in values, different mental frameworks, clashing work styles, conflicting priorities, authority issues, lack of appreciation, and more. There are also countless ways, steps, strategies, methods, and tips on how to resolve interpersonal work difficulties generally, including a vast range of interpersonal and communication skills.

Furthermore, there are several personality tests to choose from that are often used in teams and other forms of collaboration, with the idea that cooperation can be stimulated if members know their own and each other's personality type, and are able to adapt their communication accordingly.

So, what added value does Functional Fluency have over all other models, tools and methods?

One of the great advantages of Functional Fluency is that it encompasses fluid functional aspects of human functioning rather than static (personality) constructs. Functional Fluency looks at and breaks down the core of our inner reactions to others, and how effectively we respond. It helps us understand how and why we might be able to choose to move fluidly between responses in specific situations in order to invite alternative responses from ourselves and others in a congruent and authentic way. Functional Fluency is not a blueprint, rather a fluid roadmap providing you with alternate routes and options to deal effectively with complex and challenging interpersonal relationships. It is about increasing behavioural ranges, not changing who you are. Functional Fluency encourages you to try out different avenues and experiment with choices you may not allow yourself to choose.

Functional Fluency is also a common language to share, that will help you and others simplify and navigate through complex relationships within the – often complex – work context. The shared understanding associated with this common language implies that people know what it means, and know how they are expected to use it. It is concrete and practical, and focused on developing people's ability to act adequately and effectively in each given context, and to help with communication in challenging situations.

Embracing challenging interpersonal dynamics has everything to do with embracing interpersonal learning. From a leadership point of view, it is about creating a safe workplace climate where people have the space to learn about themselves and others in a co-creative way, connected in the here-and-now, finding ways together to change the narrative for the better. This too is what Functional Fluency is about.

At the end of the day, it is about how people treat each other, and how people care for themselves as total beings, resulting in desirable outcomes. This all relates to the leading questions when working with Functional Fluency:

*   How do people benefit from my behaviour?
*   Am I using my energy positively to build effective, healthy and sustainable relationships?
*   Am I achieving what matters most?
*   Are we achieving what matters most?

These leading questions apply to self, other(s), the team, the organization, society, and ultimately our planet. We therefore invite you to give yourself and others in your workplace a license to practise, permission to risk mistakes, and to learn by doing in order to develop new interpersonal strengths. We hope that the following case study and guideline will inspire you on your way.

Tip: You may find it useful to refer to the full Functional Fluency diagram (Figure 3 in Chapter 2) while reading the case study.

The story of Delivery

Case study: insights and lessons from 3 perspectives

Kim has been the CEO of Delivery, a large, growing company with branches spread over a region, for 17 years. When she started as CEO, the company had one branch with approximately 50 employees. Up till now she has been very successful in her strategy – understanding how to grow the company in a niche market. At present, the company has a central office and 10 branches with all together a little over 1200 employees.

Delivery's IT department has been a worry to her for quite a while. In the past 17 years she has seen five senior managers Finance, who were also responsible for IT, come and go. The business has been expanding exceptionally fast over the region, and she needs IT to keep up and transform to support the rapid change. After the last senior manager departed four years before, instead of hiring a new manager, Kim decided to take on a team-lead Finance and a team-lead IT who reported directly to her. Kim didn't necessarily have an affinity for IT, but she figured that she was the best person to get things going the way she wanted. The company was able to attract a professional from abroad, Lucas, with exactly the right IT credentials and experience. Just what the business needed.

Fast forward five years. Kim is increasingly having problems with Lucas. They frequently clash. Kim is dissatisfied with Lucas' performance: in recent years, Lucas has proved that he was able to introduce a few innovations into the organization successfully; however, he has not been able to meet the agreed targets and to get his team to move along with the organizational change.

In this one case[1] we will show that the interpersonal challenge is not limited to the relationship between the CEO and one of her managers. We have chosen to approach the topic of this chapter by looking at this case on three different levels through the framework of Functional Fluency. To be able to understand interpersonal difficulties in the workplace, we believe you need to have the ability to zoom in and out using a micro, meso, and macro level approach. It is often not only about the individual and their levels of behaviour, interaction, and dynamics of various kinds (micro level). It is usually worthwhile to zoom out and look at the (behavioural) dynamics on group level (meso level) and the (behaviour of a) system as a whole (macro level). The 'zoom framework' encourages the examination of interpersonal relationships from different perspectives, recognising that no one perspective alone can reveal its full complexity, and that each perspective influences the other.

The individual perspective

Setting the stage for dealing with interpersonal challenges

Kim and Lucas are in their monthly progress meeting. Kim introduces the following topic whilst slightly raising her voice: the IT plan to implement Delivery's business strategy. She asks Lucas why it is taking him so long to get the job done. Kim is clearly annoyed. This isn't the first time this has happened. In Lucas' first year on the job, she sat beside him and showed him how she wanted the plan to be drafted. She practically made the plan herself. The second and third year, Lucas wrote a plan, but twice in a row it was not what Kim expected. It was lacking vision and, as far as she could see, 'merely' stated that Lucas wanted budget to employ extra IT professionals to work on his team. Kim refused to grant this request, arguing that Lucas had insufficiently substantiated why he needed more staff. Lucas is now holding his breath and is looking down at the table. Quietly, he says that he will try to finish the plan in the next couple of weeks, but that he doesn't really have the time because he is running around putting out fires every day. That is why he needs more people on his team with other competencies than the current team members. He needs higher skilled people to take the IT team to the next level. After arguing the case for a while, Kim furiously slams her fist on the table and shouts that she is fed up with hearing about extra staff. The conversation gets extremely heated, with Kim doing almost all the talking. She ends the monologue by saying that she wants the plan on her desk by the end of the week. Lucas is now staring icily at the floor. He gets up in silence and leaves. Kim is relieved. From her point of view, the interaction has been painful, but swift. She has made her point, and is sure that Lucas has now got the message and will deliver. But before the week is over, Lucas goes on leave.

While Kim and Lucas are discussing items on the agenda, all sorts of things happen between the two of them, and within themselves; things they are not expressing towards each other and things they are not even conscious of. Individually, both have the potential to use their energy effectively, using the Golden Five, and in many other contexts they do. However when interacting together, they repeatedly leak energy into less effective behaviour, the Purple Pitfalls. Using this example, we will first zoom in on individual (patterns of) behaviour.

Behaviour – inter-and intrapersonal

Your behaviour is about what you do and how you do it, how you act towards certain stimuli, how you talk to or conduct yourself (intrapersonal) or relate to others in any situation (interpersonal). While this behaviour is often obvious – such as slamming a fist on the table – often it is barely visible to others or even yourself, for example whether you are breathing fast or slowly, tightening your jaw, or experiencing a positive or negative internal dialogue.

'Functionally Fluent' behaviour refers to connections flowing smoothly. This works on two levels:

1 Between you and others (interpersonal): your behaviour helps the communication between you and others flow seamlessly, making you capable of connecting effectively.
2 Within yourself (intrapersonal): in order to connect with others, you must first connect with yourself. This is easier when you have a high level of self-awareness, when your thoughts, feelings, and actions are in sync, and you are able to self-regulate.

While this may seem simple, often these aspects do not align easily, which you may recognise from your own life.[2] For example, a manager who often makes time to help his colleagues because he believes it is important to give support, but internally feels irritated with them, especially when they don't show appreciation. Sometimes it can be impossible to align and regulate your thoughts, feelings and emotions, causing your behaviour to stop being fluent and your connection with others to become more difficult. In most challenging situations your behaviour can become an obstacle to achieving the things that are important to you.

Neither Kim's nor Lucas' thoughts, feelings, and actions are in sync and the quality of the connection between the two of them, as well as within themselves, is, to say the least, very poor. The evidence lies in the lack of use of the Golden Five and the amount of energy they are both unconsciously putting into (a combination of) Purple Pitfall behaviour. Kim's visible behaviour can be considered as Dominating and Immature, and Lucas' behaviour as Compliant/Resistant.

After separately being introduced to the Functional Fluency model and their own personal TIFF© profiles[3], both Kim and Lucas realise that they are lacking awareness of the vast amount of energy that they are using ineffectively in the context of their working relationship and even beyond.

As mentioned before, in order to connect with others, you must first connect with yourself. To be able to connect with yourself, you need to be 'with it' and in tune with your own internal states, as well as sensitive and receptive to stimuli from others and the environment. Being grounded, alert and aware are three out of six key behavioural characteristics of Accounting, central in the Functional Fluency model. Kim and Lucas both need to do the necessary Accounting as a first step to restoring the connection with themselves and each other.

When you are at your most effective, you take account of the various aspects of yourself, other people, and what is happening in the world around you. Important Accounting functions include assessing what is relevant in a situation, working out what is significant in the circumstances, imagining possible implications, and considering what needs to be decided. Then comes the choosing of options and necessary conditions for action to take place. All of this uses energy internally, 'head, heart and gut', which is why we say that Accounting works like an internal 'mode of behaviour' i.e. it is not observable.[4]

Accounting, therefore, is what a person does internally in order to choose what to do or say next. It is an internal activity that allows you to act in an emotionally intelligent way, and to be effective in your relationships with others.[5] When you fail to do this in challenging situations, difficulties are likely to arise.

It may be helpful to introduce the term 'Discounting' here. 'Discounting' is an internal mechanism which involves people minimizing or ignoring some aspect of themselves, others, or the reality of the situation.[6] Discounting is the process by which we unwittingly fail to notice something, recognise its significance, or take necessary action in relation to it. It is about ignoring crucial information needed to get a resolution. One of the key characteristics of discounting the way we are talking about here, is that it is done out of awareness. In the example above, the manager who often helps others is discounting the stress he is feeling due to not getting round to his own work, and also the trigger that is causing him to put the interest of others before his own. Discounting is a common reaction when we encounter new and/or stressful situations. Through Accounting we can discover what we are discounting.

Kim's story

What could Kim and Lucas possibly be ignoring? Or in other words, what should they be taking into account? Let's begin with Kim. The Accounting process she goes through starts off with distancing herself from the hectic pace of the day, turning off the stimuli around her, so she can ground herself: deepening her breathing, with two feet on the ground, acknowledging all her senses, literally and figuratively calming, and slowing down to get more in touch with her internal and external world. Grounding gives Kim space to notice the reality externally and internally as it is presenting itself to her (alert) and helps her to recognise, realise and register in order to make sense of what is going on (aware). Like most of us, the challenge for Kim is to do all of this without labelling or judging – as we tend to want to label everything as "good" or "bad" or "right" or "wrong" – and by being present, without ruminating on the past or worrying about the future. Here is a glimpse of some things that come up for Kim:

Whilst becoming intentionally still, Kim feels a sudden surge of emotion in herself. She can feel her heart beating stronger and tears coming to her eyes. By slowing down her breath, she can give space to the emotions, feelings and thoughts that are emerging. What is the reality that is presenting itself to her?

Kim has managed to run the business successfully for years, but now she is feeling a lack of confidence, anxious and stressed, and is having more outbursts than she 'functionally' allows herself to have. She has played an important part in initiating the expansion and major change the business is going through. Advised by Lucas, she had decided to make a huge investment in a new IT technology to connect processes, systems, and data needed to optimise the operations. Lucas and his team are not living up to her expectations, and a lot is at stake. Experts are flying in from abroad, and an additional project team has been installed to help with the implementation. The costs are getting way out of control, and soon she will have to report to the shareholders of the business. Kim is finding it hard to relax in her free time and is having sleepless nights. In the daytime she feels nervous and gets easily irritated. Kim's 'solution' up till now has been to micromanage and rigidly keep on pressuring Lucas to produce a plan the way she wants it, but without success.

What is going on looking through the lens of Functional Fluency?

Putting energy into Accounting helps Kim see what she is doing and how she is behaving. She realises that she has been ignoring the information her own body is giving her about the impact of the stress she is under. She also realises that she is using Dominating behaviour towards Lucas. She believes it is Lucas' fault that things are getting out of hand (blaming); she is excessively telling Lucas what to do and how to do it (bossy); she is discounting Lucas' view, assuming that her own point of view is right (knowing-better); she is pointing out mistakes (fault-finding), much less than pointing out successes, and last but not least, she has recently given Lucas a very bad performance review (punitive). Showing up angry (Dominating – interpersonal) is Kim's way to cover up or not feel that she is experiencing anxiety (Compliant - intrapersonal). Although she is clearly not achieving the results she wants, she is also leaving things on the back burner, over-tolerantly waiting and waiting for Lucas to come up with the answer. She realises that there is inconsistency in her behaviour; she insists that Lucas must create a plan, and eventually lets him off the hook (Marshmallowing), due to the fact that she has many other priorities. Ultimately, she blames herself for not being able to turn the tide (Dominating), and she is finding it increasingly harder to control her emotions (Immature). She also acknowledges that she has not at all been taking into consideration Lucas' feelings and needs (lack of Nurturing), even though her HR manager has expressed her concerns several times, and Lucas has been coming to work unshaven and looking sloppy for quite a while.

What are the gains?

Kim concludes that she is not using the Being-in-Charge modes effectively. She has unconsciously been using Dominating (ineffective Guiding and Directing) and Marshmallowing behaviour (ineffective care) and too little Structuring (effective Guiding and Directing) and Nurturing (effective care) behaviour. Neither she nor Lucas are benefiting from his Purple Pitfall behaviour. And together with avoiding the reality of things (lack of Accounting), her behaviour is holding them hostage. Continuing to act in the same way will not lead to a resolution. Kim needs to let go of her ineffective Being-in-Charge behaviours so as to craft more subtle interventions using the Golden Five, with a higher chance of positive outcomes. By asking herself: 'How do I and others benefit from my actions?', she can assess the current reality. By taking into account all that is relevant, and considering which behaviour is helpful in the situation, she will be able to exert a positive influence.

Doing things differently using the Golden Five

Kim considers the combination of effective behavioural options she can choose from. She realises that she first needs to shift her perspective of herself, Lucas, and the situation by changing her own ineffective in-trapersonal dialogue. Her inner voices of judgement and fear, together with Lucas' resistant behaviour, have been triggering her to blame Lucas and ultimately herself for the undesirable situation they are in. Until now, her negative thoughts and feelings have been preventing her from connecting to reality. She lists a number of Golden Five behaviours she needs to embrace: unconditionally accept herself and Lucas (Nurturing); acknowledge reality (Accounting); admit and express her own mistakes and role (Spontaneous). Her next step will be to connect with Lucas in the here-and-now, invite him to face the hard realities together, foster resolve, and generate creative, realistic solutions to the challenges they both are encountering. She's aware that she needs to engender a sense of enough safety in Lucas, so that Lucas will be open to, and take in, a new interpersonal experience with her. This is challenging for Kim because it means she must do something she isn't used to doing. And she knows she needs to work on her capacity to hold difficult conversations considering this is indispensable for a leader.

Kim invites Lucas to meet with her outside the workplace to talk things through, and asks him to choose a place where he feels comfortable (Cooperative and Nurturing)

Kim and Lucas are sitting on a bench in beautiful green surroundings. Kim makes sure she is focused and engaged in the here-and-now. She pays attention to her breathing and is aware of her non-verbal behaviours (Accounting). With a genuine friendly voice and a smile, she thanks Lucas for coming (Cooperative). She continues by apologising for her over-controlling behaviour, and reveals (Spontaneous) that a lot has to do with the fact that she is worried about the way things are going. She understands that her behaviour has not been beneficial for Lucas, and that if she was in Lucas' shoes, she would feel awful (Nurturing). She tells Lucas that she would like to use this time together to (1) understand how he has been experiencing the past months and years and how he is feeling (Nurturing), (2) to look at the current situation together and assess the reality (Accounting) and (3) explore what they need to do next (Structuring). Lucas closes his eyes for a moment and breathes out deeply (Accounting). He feels the tension in his body slowly ease away.

By fluently putting her energy into a combination of effective behaviours (Golden Five), Kim invites Lucas to 'respond instead of react'. She is able to "hold space", meaning she is physically, mentally, and emotionally present for Lucas, offering him the opportunity to be fully seen and heard. Contrary to what Kim usually does, she verbally and non-verbally[7] walks alongside Lucas in the journey he is in, without judging him, making him feel inadequate, trying to fix him, or trying to impact the outcome. When we hold space for other people, we open our hearts, offer unconditional support, and let go of judgement and control.

We invite you to stop right here for a moment. If you have a journal or piece of paper, now would be a good time to grab it.

Reflection

No relationship exists in isolation. All our interactions, whether with one, or more people, take place in a variety of contexts – families, friendships, communities, teams, organizations, society at large and, increasingly, the global context. Like many people, you are probably dealing with a complex web of relationships in your living situation, at work, in your family, and local community. Comparing different environments can help you to gain an understanding of your own attitude and competences when relating to yourself and others. Think about specific interactions you have been or are involved in whilst walking through the following questions.

• How comfortable are you with rejecting your assumptions and biases (reactions) in order to take a holistic approach and see the big picture (Accounting)? Can you think of an example of when you did this recently?
• Are there situations in which you were unable to stay free of judgement, blame, defensiveness or emotional outbursts? What led you to react in that way?
• Are you taking into account what is happening in the context, in the world around you? Think of an example.
• In what ways do you pay attention to your own changing thoughts, feelings, and behaviour moment by moment, and take responsibility for (the outcome of) your actions?

- Think of a specific difficult relationship. Looking through the Functional Fluency framework, how do you navigate this relationship?

Examine your answers for themes. Overall, how do you feel about the 'body of evidence' you have just created? How do you see experiences in your life reflected in your answers?

As you move through these different environments, what do you conclude about the quality of your connection with yourself and others?

Reflection

The four Being-in-Charge behaviours – Structuring, Dominating, Nurturing, and Marshmallowing – relate to how we use our energy to guide and direct, and look after others and ourselves (see Figure 7.1). Being-in-Charge

Figure 7.1 Effective and ineffective ways of Being in Charge.

behaviour refers to any situation where we have a responsibility for others, either as a leader or a caregiver. It also refers to the responsibility we have towards ourselves.

Considering your roles as leader and caregiver, ask yourself:

- Who are you responsible for?
- How do you give guidance and care to others and yourself? Think of some recent examples.
- How do you wield your authority? Does this empower or dis-empower those you are responsible for? Examples?
- How effective do you think you are at Being in Charge? In what way are you contributing to positive outcomes and achieving what matters most, or not?
- Do these roles leave you energised and content, or do they overwhelm you and leave you feeling stressed, out of balance or drained of energy?

We invite you to look at Figure 7.2. Each behavioural mode has a circle in it. The circles symbolise how much energy you may be putting into the various behaviours. Imagine, the more or less energy you put into a behavioural mode, the bigger or smaller the circle gets. How much energy do you think you put into each of the four Being-in-Charge behaviours? Draw your own circles. What do you conclude from this?

Lucas' story

After Kim's outburst, Lucas starts thinking of the bad performance review she had given him a couple of weeks before. He might be in danger of losing his job if he isn't able to meet her expectations. It suddenly dawns on him that he hasn't even told his wife about it. This realisation is a genuine lightbulb moment. All at once, he feels totally calm and clearly sees that he

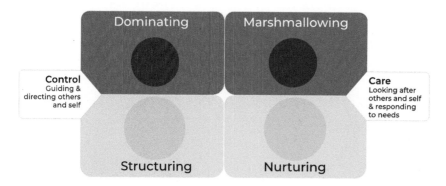

Figure 7.2 The energy you put into Being-in-Charge behaviours.

has been keeping up appearances to hide what's really going on. Lucas decides to take some time off to figure things out with help from his coach.

Lucas is feeling resistance, and acknowledges he finds it extremely confronting to look at his weak points. It is very important for Lucas to appear on top of things, telling himself and others around him that all is going well, though it is obviously not. He feels he has failed and is ashamed. He had persuaded his wife and children to come abroad with him so he could take the job as IT team lead. His wife wasn't keen and had protested, but she eventually agreed. Lucas was very excited at the beginning, and he had big plans for his team and the company.

However, he soon started to feel resistance from his team, not expecting that it would be so challenging to manage team members from a different culture. He is still afraid of getting it wrong, especially with one of the senior team members, and he feels he needs to watch his step to feel secure. Instead of finding ways to overcome the interpersonal obstacles in his team, he feels more comfortable to focus on advising the senior management team on new innovative projects. Although Kim gives him credits for his innovative ideas, Lucas felt totally pushed aside when Kim told him that she didn't want him to lead the prestigious project that he had initiated, and that he needed to focus on the IT-strategy and get his team to perform better. Also, there was no longer need for Lucas to be sitting at the senior management table.

Gradually, Lucas noticed that Kim was getting more and more irritated with him, tightening her grip, getting him to produce weekly overviews of what he was doing, focusing on details rather than the bigger picture. Lucas now realises that he hasn't been willing to acknowledge how incompetent and overwhelmed he increasingly feels in the face of Kim's demands for a detailed strategic plan, team performance improvement, her increasing control, demands from senior managers of other departments, resistance from his team, and not getting the recognition he feels he deserves. He is drinking more alcohol than before, and staying up late at night watching TV and films to distance himself from the stressors and challenges he is facing.

What is going on looking through the lens of Functional Fluency?

Looking through the lens of Functional Fluency, Lucas is able to pinpoint his ineffective behaviour. He is amazed at the amount of energy he is un- wittingly putting into Compliant/Resistant behaviour. A big trigger for Lucas is anxiety. He worries about his wife and children, about not being liked and accepted by his team, but his biggest fear is losing face (anxious). He avoids challenging his team members (placating), is not speaking up and is not showing his feelings (inhibited). Although he keeps promising Kim that he will deliver, he doesn't (defiant). He feels angry and humiliated that she hasn't given him the status and position he thinks he deserves. He 'secretly' goes against her wishes, spending a lot of time with some team members involved in the implementation of the project that he had initiated, trying to influence them to go in a certain way (rebellious). The more energy Kim is putting into Dominating behaviour, the more Lucas is putting into Compliant/Resistant behaviour.

Discovering that the dynamics he is experiencing with Kim are very similar to the dynamics he used to experience with his mother is a huge eye-opener for Lucas. He learns from his coach that if your energy slips into one or more Purple Pitfalls, you have left the present and are operating as you did as a child or as a significant person from your childhood behaved with you. This is what we call 'transference'[8]. This concept is useful when considering why you might be reacting to certain people in particular ways, for example to those in authority (as in Lucas' case), or perhaps a certain type of personality. Lucas was 'putting his mother's face onto Kim and reacting in a way that was not connected to the present.

What are the gains?

Lucas feels relieved, as if a big weight has dropped off his shoulders. By using compassionate, empathic, understanding, and accepting behaviour towards himself (Nurturing), he is in a better position to look at his Purple Pitfalls. He is relieved that he is, unlike before, able to look at his dark side without feeling bad. We are all human after all. He needed to recognise his Purple Pitfalls first before acknowledging and exploring them. Asking himself 'what in this circumstance (the trigger) is making me behave this way?' is key. He understands that this is not meant to be a judgmental and self-punishing exercise (Dominating), but a learning exercise. By observing his behaviour (Accounting), without judgement (Dominating), and with curiosity and zest (Spontaneous), he can discover the triggers that cause him to slip into his Purple Pitfalls. One of his biggest insights is his reactive behavioural pattern in this particular situation, and it starts off with anxiety (Compliant/Resistant). Instead of pushing it away by numbing himself with alcohol and binge watching (Marshmallowing), he needs to look it in the eye with acceptance and compassion (Nurturing).

Doing things differently using the Golden Five

Although he feels anxious, Lucas is aware that he needs to build up his confidence and assertiveness to have the conversation with Kim (Cooperative).

He must let go of giving Kim and his team members the blame (Dominating) for his inability to deliver the strategy and be honest about his thoughts and feelings (Spontaneous).

Lucas thanks Kim for inviting him to meet in a different setting and for starting off the conversation in such a helpful way (Cooperative). He acknowledges that he hasn't been living up to expectations and that anxiety and feelings of overwhelm have been getting in the way. He also admits that he has been feeling wronged by her (Spontaneous), and that this has prompted him to put energy into things he shouldn't be working on. He understands (Nurturing) Kim's frustration and increased controlling behaviour. He is more than willing to change his attitude and behaviour for the better, considering that he will need a different kind of support from Kim than he has been receiving until now (Cooperative). He believes that a process is ongoing that is undermining learning and change, and that together they need to explore further and figure out what is necessary (Accounting), to help him and the IT team to harness their power to grow and develop together.

The conversation on the bench is a turning point in their relationship for the better. Through Accounting, both Kim and Lucas have assessed what is relevant and significant in the situation. Energy that is going into the Purple Pitfalls is not free to be spent on effective behaviour (Golden Five) that is supportive towards finding a solution to the problem, and dealing with the situation. Anxiety and stress are taking a toll on their well-being. They need to shift their energy from Purple Pitfalls to the Golden Five, take charge of their own thoughts, feelings and emotions and the situation, and connect with each other positively; otherwise the consequences could be disastrous.

Reflection

The four Being-an-Individual behaviours – Cooperative, Spontaneous, Compliant/ Resistant, and Immature – relate to how you use energy on your own behalf, how you express yourself as the person you are – both in your own unique way and in getting along with others – and how this impacts your environment (Figure 7.3).

Take a moment to reflect on the situations in which you are engaging with others as an individual in the context of the roles you have at work. Maybe you would also like to extend your reflection to other roles in your life. Ask yourself:

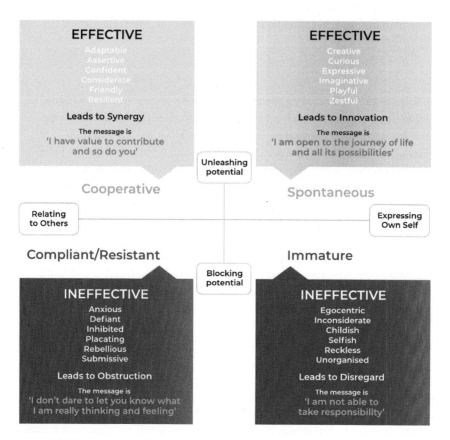

Figure 7.3 Effective and Ineffective Behaviours as an Individual.

- How well do you relate to and get along with these people? Examples?
- Do you generally have difficulties in your interactions with certain people? What is happening (behaviours) in the interaction? Is there a recognisable pattern here for you in terms of other times and other relationships?
- How do you express yourself? In which situations and with whom are you able to voice your concerns or needs to protect yourself, in a constructive manner? How does this come about?
- How is your behaviour experienced by others? Does it lead to good or bad outcomes? Can you think of examples?
- Do you feel energised or drained after engaging with others? What is happening in the interaction when you feel energised? And when you feel drained?

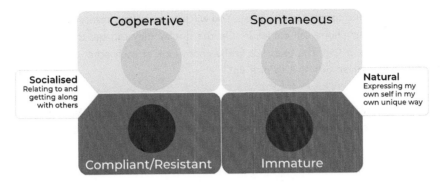

Figure 7.4 The Energy you put into Being-an-Individual behaviours.

How much energy do you think you use in the four Being-an-Individual behaviours? Draw your own circles in the diagram (Figure 7.4). What do you conclude from this?

The group perspective

The leader taking the group behaviour and dynamics into account

It's Monday morning, 8 am, and Julia, Maria, Sebastián and Mateo are sitting behind their desks. They are exchanging stories about their weekend and joking around whilst peering over the tops of the office partition panels that are used to separate their workstations. Lucas walks in with Anne, both returning from a meeting concerning one of the new projects. It immediately falls quiet in the room. Lucas says good morning and sits down at his desk. It remains silent in the room. After a while he slides on his chair back from behind his panel and says to Mateo who is sitting in the workstation next to him: "Thank you for responding separately to the message I sent over the weekend in our team's WhatsApp group. Mateo, question, how are you all getting along with setting up the issue log and recording your time sheets? I really do need this information for the team's strategy plan." Mateo glances at his colleagues who are all looking down, and he apologetically answers that they have all been too busy to log and register. The phone starts ringing frequently. Mateo is the one who picks up, until he is called away to help with a problem in a different department. Lucas and Anne leave to go to another project meeting. A phone call comes in from another department and Julia answers … "No sorry I can't help you. You will have to ask our manager about that." Another phone call comes in. On the display they can see that their CEO, Kim, is calling. The ones left in the room look at each other and Julia says: "OK, whose turn is it to pick up?"

This is a snapshot of behaviour and dynamics in the IT team. We will use this example to zoom in on the patterns of group behaviour in the team.

Group behaviour and dynamics

Group dynamics[9] is a term that is used to describe the interactions, attitudes, and behaviours between a group of people who are working together. Group dynamics define how effective your team is going to be in their work performance and development. Even if your team consists of world-class professionals, when group dynamics are poor, the result of their collaboration will be far from perfection.

The process of being influenced by the group as a whole is subtle and multi-layered. Groups influence our behaviour, our thoughts, and our energy (emotions, needs and physical sensations). The most obvious and concrete layer of influence is the layer of *visible behaviour*. The quality of the interaction between the members (behaviour) determines the extent to which the available energy is directed towards the team's task.[10] When team members are unaware of their Purple Pitfalls in certain contexts and situations, they cannot help but react to each other. Interpersonal challenges in a group are extremely difficult to overcome when people are unaware of how they themselves are preventing the resolution of problematic situations through their own ineffective or less effective behaviour and haven't yet learned how to use their energy effectively for a better outcome. It is all about mastering the use of our energy effectively on behalf of self and others.

In general, it is difficult to get a grip on what is going on under the surface, and how the group is influencing individual members' attitudes and behaviours. However, using the Functional Fluency framework will help identify both the effective and ineffective behaviour and behavioural patterns in the team, and bring coherence as well as disruptions to the surface.

What is going on looking through the lens of Functional Fluency?

Together with his coach, Lucas takes time to reflect on his behaviour and interaction with the team. He is neglecting to involve his team members in the change and new projects but tells them what to do (Dominating) and expects them to follow. He is creating a lot of work for his team by not saying no to senior management. He should be the boundary keeper for his team, but is struggling with keeping boundaries (Marshmallowing) and setting clear and consistent expectations and limits (Structuring). He has formed a positive relationship with his compatriot Anne, and they work well together (Cooperative). He is focusing on the task, rather than investing in building relationships in his team. Points of social connection with Julia, Maria, Sebastian, and Mateo are lacking. He hasn't taken time to get to know them, to understand the culture of their country, their needs, and viewpoints (Nurturing, Cooperative, and Spontaneous). He is managing them as though they are identical, not considering that they all need a different approach from him and need to be seen and valued as they are (Nurturing). A lot of the time Lucas is focusing on the negative and not on the positive (Dominating). Successes are not being celebrated in the team.

Team members do their very best to deliver on (short- and mid-term) projects that they know are important to the CEO (Compliant). However, team members are unresponsive (Resistant) to Lucas' efforts to bring up the team's performance. Lucas (internally) blames Julia for influencing her colleagues and blames his team for not giving him the necessary input for him to develop and implement the IT strategy (Dominating). In team meetings, Anne generally goes along with Lucas. It is Julia who is very critical of Lucas' ideas and argues, whilst others stay silent (Compliant/ Resistant). When asked for their opinion, Maria, Sebastian, and Mateo simply agree with Julia. Outside of meetings, Mateo is responsive to Lucas' requests (Cooperative). It has come to a point that Lucas is only communicating through Mateo to get things done from Julia, Maria, and Sebastian. In the meantime, Mateo is taking on way too much work, unwittingly rescuing his colleagues (Compliant and Marshmallowing).

There is an "Us vs Them" mentality in the team – a lot based on stereotyping – and Mateo has put himself in between.

What are the gains?

Lucas realises that he himself is a big contributor to the interpersonal challenges and poor group dynamics he is encountering in his team. His primary focus should be on creating the necessary conditions (effective Being-in-Charge behaviours) to improve the quality of the interaction of the group and help the team forward, instead of only focusing on the team's task. He needs to listen to his team members, see and value them as they are, and take the different needs and viewpoints into account (Nurturing). Providing appropriate structure and boundaries, and setting clear and consistent limits and priorities (Structuring), are necessary for his team to feel secure enough to explore, grow, and learn (Spontaneous). He needs to build up his confidence and skills of diplomacy and assertiveness

(Cooperative) in order to handle the cultural diversity in his team effectively. He knows that playfulness is a good way to connect with his team members as it is an important part of their culture (Spontaneous). Lucas is aware that he is at a stage of unconscious incompetence, and that it will take time and consistent effort to incorporate the Golden Five behaviours into his daily working life (Structuring). This will be crucial to building trust and a safe and inclusive learning environment for his team.

Doing things differently using the Golden Five

Lucas begins with having one-on-ones with each team member to find out what they are truly thinking and feeling about their day-to-day work, his leadership, the team, and the organization, and what their needs are (Nurturing). It feels very risky for Lucas to do this, considering the current reality. However – previously role-modelled by Kim - choosing to first express his own thoughts and feelings and share his insights about the impact of his own ineffective behaviour opens the way for each team member to speak about what was previously kept quiet (Spontaneous). He uses an image of the Functional Fluency model, and playfully indicates to each of his team members what he has been doing, explaining about his Purple Pitfalls and what he needs to do less of and what he needs to do more of (Structuring). This helps team members to also recognise the dysfunctional behaviours and dynamics in the team. As a next step, Lucas organises one of the first (out of office) team retreats with the intention to work, reflect, play, tap into passions, interests and potential, and strengthen team relationships (Golden Five).

> It is a couple of weeks after the team retreat. Julia has suggested they implement agile working so that the team can better manage and organise their projects (Cooperative). Agile roles and responsibilities have been divided in the team (Structuring). The team is standing around the whiteboard they have put up in their workspace to visualise the work that needs to be done as a team, and they are having fun whilst having their newly introduced weekly stand-up meeting (Spontaneous). Together they define the tasks for the week and divide them amongst themselves (Cooperative), and Lucas checks that the workload isn't too much and that the tasks are evenly divided (Structuring). Sebastian looks around the room and says: "what a relief that we have had the office partition panels taken away. Thank you for taking care of that Lucas, they were really bothering us".

The one-on-ones and the team retreat provide Lucas with a great deal of information, which he shares with Kim. Based on that information, Kim and Lucas have reason to believe that it is necessary to look beyond the boundaries of the team and take the organizational context into consideration to discover what else needs to be done to strengthen the team and improve teamwork.

Reflection

It's important to understand your team behaviours and dynamics and the part that you play, so that you can use your insights to manage your team in a more effective way. Think of a team that you are currently working with or have worked with in the past. Bring the team members' and your own behaviours into your awareness. Ask yourself the following questions and write down what comes up for you using the Functional Fluency framework. Be specific about what people (including yourself) are doing when interacting (verbally and non-verbally):

- What are the energy gains (Golden Five) and energy drains (Purple Pitfalls) in the context of team behaviour and dynamics?
- What behaviours do you see when the team is together? Who is responding to who/what (Golden Five)? Who is reacting to who/what (Purple Pitfalls)? What is the outcome?
- Who are getting along well with each other and who aren't? How can you tell?
- What behaviours in the team are helpful towards achieving the team's task? What behaviours are getting in the way?
- What combination of Golden Five behaviours can you and your team use to improve the team dynamics?

Organizational perspective

The leader taking the system into account

Kim and her senior management team are having an Accounting session about the IT-situation in the context of the organization. They have scheduled the entire morning for this. Kim has asked an external facilitator to guide the process as she knows that she tends to overpower her colleagues in meetings resulting in people clamming up. They are having a constructive conversation, and acknowledge that this usually happens when they are talking about strategic issues. Patricia, head of Marketing, is the first to make a critical remark, opening the conversation. "Let's face it, we all say that IT is an essential enabler to the successful implementation of the strategy, but it is always the last agenda item in our meetings, and we only briefly pay attention to issues if there is any time left". Deirdre, head of Communication, continues: "I agree, and as long as I have been sitting around this table, which is seven years now, IT has always been the poor relation". Kim, your portfolio expanded when you decided to take on Finance and IT. You have a lot on your plate. "Yes, and so have all of us", Colin, head of Operations, adds. I notice that we are all pushing a huge number of IT-related projects into Lucas' tunnel as we all want to achieve our mid-term goals we have agreed upon with Kim. Because Lucas never says 'no' he is creating expectations he cannot fulfil. Deirdre looks at Kim and daringly asks: "Does our management team take 'no' for an answer? You need to come up with good arguments why something cannot be done around here".

Behaviour, systems thinking and organizational culture

This section links to the previous section about interpersonal processes in a team, within the broader context of organizational life and culture. An organization is best understood as a whole, rather than in parts. An individual is part of a team. The team is part of a department. The department is part of a business unit, and so on. Nothing members of an organization or a team do happens in a vacuum. As with any ecosystem, interdependency is the key to a smooth-running operation in an organization or team, with each function feeding another. Within systems thinking we consider people, teams, and organizations as systems where the individual parts are interdependent. The quality of the relationships and connections between those parts determine the actual strength as well as the organizational culture. The workplace culture is in fact a system.

The interpersonal tensions and conflicts we encounter in organizations and teams are often reflections of unresolved issues in the wider system around them. Every organization has a system that guides the behaviour of the people. If you focus on the people with problematic behaviour, then you only see the symptom carriers. Sometimes, difficult interpersonal relationships become a lightning rod for larger issues in the workplace. Although these workplace tensions are presented to us as interpersonal issues (at small group level), often, larger systemic issues are at the root of the problem.

Of course, many problems are not systemic. However, in the case of pattern repetition, it becomes relevant to look systemically at what is going on; instead of looking at difficult interpersonal relationships in a vacuum, zoom out to macro level and treat them as a means to understand the deeper problematic themes that may be present within the larger organization.

You can probably imagine that it is extremely challenging to get a grip on how the system is influencing behaviour and the organizational culture. However, also on this level, using the Functional Fluency framework can help identify Purple Pitfalls and Golden Five within a system, and whether or not the system is contributing towards a positive, trusting, inclusive organizational culture in which people can thrive.

What is going on through the lens of Functional Fluency?

The Accounting session gives the SMT insight into the 'behaviour of the system'. Although difficult to digest, they acknowledge that a disproportionate amount of energy is unconsciously going into Dominating, Marshmallowing, and Immature behaviour within the organizational context, which in turn triggers the IT team into mainly Compliant/Resistant behaviour. Starting with Immature: a silo mentality deters cross-department collaboration and organizational goals from being achieved, management of projects and priorities are far from organised, senior management is pressuring Lucas and the IT team for quick wins, and employees expect the IT team to stand ready for any IT-related issue without taking responsibility for their own IT-learning and competencies. The CEO has a Dominating/Marshmallowing leadership style: she has a need for control and has difficulty delegating. She individually manages the other senior managers and tells them what to do. They in turn comply. Judging, fault-finding, and criticising are common, causing anxiety in the organization.

If we were to list all systemic behaviours in this chapter, we would need many more pages. Figure 7.5[11] aims to simplify the complexity and give you a better understanding of the behaviours and interaction between the team and its environment. It shows that there is currently too much ineffective behaviour (purple) and too little effective behaviour (golden) within the context of the team, and how the team is currently reacting, thinking, and feeling (purple) as opposed to how the team could be responding, thinking, and feeling (golden).

What are the gains?

Kim and the senior managers are happy they are having this conversation now, and not later. They need to come up with better thinking as a team. They have a choice: either they stay with the system and culture that has unconsciously been created, and the concepts that embody them (features of their current daily working life), or they challenge them through Accounting in order to co-create new helpful meanings in the present. They acknowledge that the current system is far too task-oriented, over-controlling, and that this is causing compliance and resistance in the organization. This in turn inhibits the co-creative and innovative forces in the IT team and in the

1. **ISSUE:** What is needed to increase the adaptability of the IT team, so that the team can meet current expectations of the organization and innovate for tomorrow?

2. CONTEXT:

Too much / many:
- silo mentality (Immature)
- over-tolerance for recurring IT-related issues in all parts of the organization (Marshmallowing)
- complaints from internal clients and reliance on IT (Immature)
- projects that IT needs to be involved in (Immature)
- priorities/emergency work (Immature)
- urge for quick wins (Immature)
- requests from senior managers (Immature)
- control and micro-management from CEO (Dominating and Marshmallowing)
- role and responsibility overload for one person (Marshmallowing)
- judging and criticisms (Dominating)

Too little:
- attention for IT at senior management level (Structuring and Nurturing)
- collaboration across boundaries (Cooperation)
- managerial coordination in the organization at tactical level (Structuring and Cooperative)
- delegation of roles and responsibilities by the CEO (Structuring)
- clarity re distribution of roles and responsibilities between line manager and staff (Structuring)
- influence or say in matters affecting the team (Cooperative)
- support to improve IT skills, increase IT capacity, and to create cultural competence (Structuring and Nurturing)
- reflection and room to learn and improve (Accounting)
- psychological safety (Nurturing and Structuring) to express thoughts, feelings, and ideas (Spontaneous)
- "obligation" to dissent (Cooperative)

Ambiguous:
- what and how the organization should contribute to facilitate the needs of the team
- unspoken expectations of what the team should contribute to the achievement of organizational objectives and client value
- directive management style and expecting the team to self-manage and innovate

3. TEAM ICEBERG

Current situation	Desired situation
What is the team currently doing?	**What is the desired behaviour?**
• working individually, putting out fires • resisting adapting to changing needs • resisting getting the facts straight: what are our clients' needs? How many issues are recurring and how much time is this costing us? • placating and avoiding conflicts (in team and also with others in the organization) • withdrawing and complaining • criticizing team lead • not speaking up • judging and criticisms	• listening and being curious about each other • showing initiative • getting the facts straight • taking responsibility for learning • expressing needs and ideas freely • making matters negotiable and breaking traditional rules of conduct, including towards management • looking beyond team boundaries
What is the team currently thinking?	**What is the team currently thinking?**
• we must make do with what we have • our opinion doesn't count, we don't have any influence • our team lead is causing us more work because he hasn't got the competence to solve things himself • we're not involved in the planning of new projects, so we can't help it if mistakes are made • it is too risky to address others on their behaviour	• we have confidence in our own ability • Accounting is self-evident • we can deal with ambiguity and contradictions • we provide added value at all times • we know it is important that we do the right things for the right reasons
What is the team currently feeling?	**Which feeling should be prevailing?**
• we don't belong in the workplace • we feel worthless • we are afraid of doing something wrong • everyone for themselves	• we are motivated and prepared to gain experience through practice and experiential learning • we are important • we have a high sense of self-esteem

Figure 7.5 Interactions between the team and its environment.

organization (Cooperative and Spontaneous). The real challenges in the organization are not in the parts or the people but in the connections. Building effective interpersonal connections is key. Fostering the ability to understand and accept (Nurturing) and to speak up and share feelings with each other (Spontaneous), is necessary to give rise to bonding and new interpersonal and collective learning and meaning. The focus of the leader and the managers should be on enabling the collaboration across boundaries and improving the quality of interaction at all levels of the organization, starting with themselves as role models.

Doing things differently using the Golden Five

Kim and her management team become extremely motivated to transform the organizational culture into a "Golden Five" culture. It means taking on a new perspective and sense of ownership that cuts across silos and improves the ability to collaborate across boundaries.

First, they need to change their actions in order to change their current beliefs and values that have led to behaviours that in turn have shaped the Purple Pitfall organizational culture. They realise that a whole-system change begins with a shift in the personal consciousness of individuals. The organization won't change if the people don't change, and the change must begin with the personal transformation of the leadership group[12]. The SMT decides to create a learning culture in Delivery. Accounting and individual and collective learning must become a priority in the organization and conditions for this to take place need to be created through Structuring and Nurturing.

As leaders of the organization, they need to consistently drive the process, be committed, and become exemplars of the Golden Five behaviours they want to see reflected in every aspect of the organization's structures, systems, processes and interpersonal connections.[13] They are aware that this will take discipline, acceptance, and patience, one step at a time. In the short term they organise several sessions to create an interrelated IT company strategy. They introduce programme management, focusing on project interdependencies. This enables them to prioritise with the available resources, identify obstacles, consider ways to remove them, and engage the entire IT team in the process (Structuring). They also take steps to build a foundation of psychological safety (which was lacking in the organization). Through listening, empathising, valuing, and inviting differing views (Nurturing), team members are encouraged to be candid, ask questions often and early, and share worries and needs (Spontaneous). Senior leaders start showing that people can freely admit mistakes (senior leaders first) without fear of retribution. Being-in-Charge effectively is crucial to create a secure environment for optimal learning.

Lucas and the IT team are having their quarterly feed-forward session with the senior managers. The SMT has been strengthened by the appointment of Sofia, the new Information manager responsible for IT and innovation. An operational IT manager has been added to the IT team and Lucas has taken on the role of IT programme manager. Kim begins with the check in: "How is everyone feeling today?". Anything that needs to be addressed first for you all to be present? She then passes the baton to Sofia to lead the session: "I want to spend the next 45 minutes reflecting on how we're all managing the changes. Specifically, are there any challenges, uncertainties, tensions? What kind of support do you need? What questions do we need to answer? Are there any stories you want to check out? Anything we need to explore further together ...".

Reflection

In closing, we invite you to explore any challenging interpersonal relationship you are currently experiencing or have experienced in the past and consider how the context may have influenced it. Ask yourself the following questions using the Functional Fluency framework:

- What is the problem and who is involved?
- How are stakeholders in the organizational system interacting?
- With what behaviour and patterns of interaction are stakeholders unconsciously maintaining the undesired situation?
- Which systemic issues are at the root of the problem?
- What behaviour does the system need more and less of to achieve what matters most?

Be mindful that there is no wrong or right. It is not about apportioning blame, but about revealing patterns of interaction and underlying themes that are at the root of the problem.

Last but not least, it is important that you look at your own and others' behaviour with mildness. We all make mistakes, and we all slip into Purple Pitfalls now and then. The point is to recognise, acknowledge, accept and embrace reality, get back on track using the Functional Fluency Golden Five and celebrate!

Summary

- Functional Fluency enables us to resolve challenging situations from three perspectives: individual, group and organization

- Functionally fluent behaviour refers to connections flowing smoothly at both the intrapersonal and interpersonal level
- Difficult interpersonal relationships affect not only the people involved but also their teams and the organization
- Energy that is going into the Purple Pitfalls is not free to be spent on effective behaviour (Golden Five) that is supportive towards resolving the situation
- A difficult interpersonal relationship within a group or team may be caused by poor group dynamics
- The Functional Fluency framework helps identify effective and ineffective behavioural patterns in the team which can be addressed by a combination of Golden Five behaviours
- Larger systemic issues may be at the root of difficult interpersonal relationships and workplace tensions which are labelled as interpersonal issues
- For leaders, using Structuring and Nurturing behaviours effectively is key to creating a safe workplace climate where people can learn about themselves and others co-creatively
- Transforming a Purple Pitfall organizational culture into a Golden Five culture takes time, commitment, patience, and consistency of leadership

Notes

1 This case is drawn from our own coaching experience, with details changed to safeguard anonymity
2 Koopmans, L. (2014). *Functional Fluency, een introductie*, Strook Tijdschrift voor Transactionele Analyse, themanummer p. 21.
3 The TIFF© tool provides individuals, teams, and organizations insight into how to effectively use energy in a way that behaviour is beneficial to self and others and that goals that truly matter are achieved. TIFF© is used in personal and professional development by leaders, managers, consultants, coaches, counsellors, mentors, teachers, and psychotherapists to raise morale, develop emotional literacy and empower behavioural change.
4 Temple, S. (2016). *Key Understandings for Using the Functional Fluency Model*, IP Papers/FF & TIFF Theory into Practice Alerts/5c.
5 Ibid.
6 Schiff, J. et al. (1975) *The Cathexis Reader*, Longman.
7 Your nonverbal communication cues—the way you listen, look, move, and react—tell the person you're communicating with whether or not you care, if you're being truthful, and how well you're listening. When your nonverbal signals match up with the words you're saying, they are aligned with the Golden Five which increases trust, clarity, and rapport. When they aren't aligned, they can generate tension, mistrust, and confusion.
8 The concept of transference emerged from Sigmund Freud's psychoanalytic practice in the 1890s.
9 Kurt Lewin coined the term group dynamics in 1939. He defined group dynamics as "positive and negative forces within groups of people". It means that each group has its own psychological climate that influenced behaviour and

performance. Moreover, each personality involved in the group unconsciously sets the direction of group dynamics, whether it's positive or negative. See Lewin, K. (1948), *Resolving social conflicts; selected papers on group dynamics* (1935–1946). Gertrude W. Lewin (ed.). New York: Harper and Row.

10 Jong, de J. (2021). *Competente mensen. Incompetente teams*, Boom Uitgevers Amsterdam.

11 The image is based on the Functional Analysis model that has been derived from The Michigan (stress) model, (Kahn et al., 1964) a model that describes how characteristics of the work environment can lead to stress or illness in employees and to help people who are experiencing stress understand what is involved. The Michigan model has been adapted by Marijke Lingsma for practical application in coaching processes. See Kahn, R.L., Wolfe, D.M., Quinn, R.P., Snoek, J.D., & Rosenthal, R.A. (1964). *Organizational stress: studies in role conflict and ambiguity*. New York: Wiley, and Broers, A., en Lingsma, M. (2018). De 10 principes van Agile-Lean Team coaching. Zelforganiserend verbeteren in praktijk. Boom Uitgevers, Amsterdam.

12 Barret, R. (2006). Building a values-driven Organization. A whole System Approach to Cultural Transformation. Routledge, New York.

13 Ibid.Suggested extra reading: Kegan R & Laskow Lahey, L. (2009). *Immunity to change. How to overcome it and unlock the potential in yourself and your organization*, Harvard Business Press, Boston, Massachusetts.

Chapter 8

Using Functional Fluency to support Organizational Development and Transformational Change

Paul Robinson

Introduction

In this chapter, we'll take a look at how the Functional Fluency model can support transformational change in organisations. Although Functional Fluency is focused on supporting better and more appropriate inter-personal communications, it can be used to great advantage to support an organizational change process or an organizational development pro-gramme, through enabling, facilitating, and supporting better and more emotionally intelligent, inter-personal communications on a much larger scale.

Most of my experience in leading organizational development and change programmes have been from within the organization that is going through the process, with some experience of being an external change agent as well. Most of this has been within the not-for-profit sector (local government, charities and third sector organizations). So this chapter is written mostly from an internal-change-agent perspective. Working as an external change agent is a little different: mostly from the perspective of needing to gather more information at the start of the process, to become familiar with the culture and processes of the organization and to be sure that the resources available are sufficient to achieve the objectives of the change. And, of course, there is less experience of working with the people in the organiza-tion – which impacts on communications.

There are many models of organizational change processes, and many books have been written about the various ways of planning and im-plementing a change process. They all have some common features, so I'll use a generic model developed by Jack Mezirow[1] that I am familiar with, and use in many different contexts to support transformational change, as a vehicle to explore how Functional Fluency can support organisational change.

Organizational change is always a challenging process, due to the re-sistance to the change process that is inevitably generated because change generates uncertainty and unpredictability. People in organizations that are

DOI: 10.4324/9781003345527-8

committing to change can often become scared and withdrawn, or go into denial and resist the change process because they are comfortable doing what they do in the way that they do it. They face a situation that they are unfamiliar with, which presents them with a dilemma: "what should I do?" Organizational development programmes are less scary, but they may also generate a level of distrust and speculation, as some employees may view this as a precursor to an organizational change process.

Mezirow terms this period of indecision and confusion a "disorienting dilemma", and his solution is to support a transformational learning process that then facilitates a transformational change in behaviour. This process applies equally to an organization and to individuals as, at the end of the change process, the organization has learned how to do whatever it does, differently. The organizational culture and its norms have changed.

Organizational change processes are focused on problem solving (on a large scale), and the best solutions come from identifying the cause of the problem and finding a good solution for that, rather than working on the effects of the problem. Functional Fluency supports individuals within the organization to account for reality and to making appropriate choices, whilst also accounting for the potential responses of the people affected by the action. This is where the Golden Five aspects of Functional Fluency are so useful, and why Functional Fluency is a great model to use to support and direct an organizational change process. If we are Accounting for reality and aware of the problem(s) that we want to address, we will be enquiring about the possible options, evaluate them from a rational perspective, whilst also being alert to the possible resistant responses, and we will be grounded when we make our choices. Some aspects of Co-creative Transactional Analysis (CCTA) also help staying in Accounting behaviours and avoiding (purple) pitfalls, and we'll explore this model later in the chapter.

Using Functional Fluency to support the organizational change process

Functional Fluency supports emotional intelligence: the building of better, more productive relationships through relevant, and more open, communications. Within an organizational setting, communications from managers and leaders are received by many people, all of whom have different experiences and, therefore, the potential to interpret the communications in different ways. In a time of organizational change, this potential is exacerbated as employees may already be anxious and moving towards Compliant or Resistant behaviours, and may be suspicious about communications relating to the change process. I encountered a number of organizational change processes before I became a manager, and I recall many discussions in our office about "the hidden agenda" with people often speculating about "what's not being said?"

Good communication is not just dependent on what is sent from the sender, but how it is interpreted by the receiver. When communicating with just one person, the sender can account for their past experiences of communicating with the recipient, and adjust the content of the communication accordingly. This gets increasingly difficult when communicating with a group of individuals. When leading or managing organizations or extensive teams within organizations, it becomes virtually impossible to account for all of the ways that the communication can be interpreted, when we are communicating with people that we have no experience of direct communication with. A different strategy is needed!

In these circumstances, good communications are dependent on the message being clear, so that the message received is what was intended. This is where Functional Fluency helps – at both the communication formulation stage (sender) and the interpretation stage (receiver). Earlier chapters in this book provide details about the model itself and how it supports better communications between individuals. Other chapters consider the wider use of Functional Fluency and how learning about the model supports better communications. A programme introducing employees in an organization to the model and, in particular, how to be on the look out for, and stay out of, unhelpful behaviours and responses, can significantly support a more positive organizational development and/or change process. These don't need to be extensive or protracted programmes; an hour or two with groups of individuals across the organization, or with individual teams, can significantly help to improve communications, both from the sender's and the receiver's perspectives.

To support both of these stages (sending clear communications and receiving them without negative bias), building trustful, open and respectful relationships is the key.

Reflection

Before we get into the detail, let's take a little time out to reflect on your own experience of organizational development and change processes, whether that's been from a management perspective or from being affected by a change process.

What sort of resistance have you experienced, either personally or observed in others, within an organizational change process? Can you identify any "sticky" points in the change processes?

Now, see if you can identify any miscommunication or lack of communication that contributed to the emergent difficulties. Make some notes about what went wrong and what might have avoided the difficulties that ensued, so that you can come back to them later in the chapter. Finally, see if you can relate the changes to any of the Golden Five behaviours. Again, I suggest you make some notes.

Using effective behaviours to support managing and leading the change process

In this section, I'll focus on how effective behaviours can be used by leaders and managers to support building positive relationships in organizations, and inviting clear and meaningful communications with the people affected by a change process. In the next section, I'll explain Mezirow's transformational change process and how CCTA can support staying in the effective behaviours. Having set the foundations, the final section is a case study of one significant change process that I led in a large, multi-faceted organization, to show how Functional Fluency can be used to support positive communications at different parts of the change process.

Accounting

The key characteristics of Accounting behaviours are: alert, aware, evaluative, grounded, enquiring and rational.

Accounting behaviours help to keep us in the "here and now", with the focus being on what's really going on? What information do we need? How are people responding to the process? How is it affecting them? Have we properly identified the source(s) of the issues, or are we focused on the effects? Have we considered all of the options? What are we missing? Are we staying alert to the possibility for us to slip into some of the Purple Pitfall behaviours?

- In Functional Fluency terms, these translate into the leader being alert to signs of distress in those most affected by the changes, and aware of the levels of anxiety that may be generated by the uncertainty that accompanies change.
- Leaders need to be regularly evaluating the impact that the change processes are having on the people working in the organization, and Accounting for this by responding positively with actions that can ameliorate the impact.
- We need to stay grounded in the here and now and avoid over speculating, whilst also having contingency plans for responding appropriately to issues, if and when they emerge.
- Accessing our curiosity and enquiring about employees' thoughts and feelings, as the process progresses, and inviting feedback and questions, provides useful information that keeps us informed about how the process is going.
- Staying rational and grounded in the here and now and giving ourselves time to think of appropriate responses to situations as they arise, instead of reacting quickly and inappropriately will pay dividends in the longer term. We need to avoid making promises that we can't be sure that we

can keep! I recall a local councillor, at a public meeting to discuss proposals for revitalising an area of terraced housing, stating that "there would be houses demolished over his dead body"! He lost his credibility following the demolition of two rows of houses (and he was not found underneath the rubble!).

It is essential to stay focussed on what is actually occurring, rather than what we expect to be happening, and we need to adjust our responses and actions to account for the reality of the situation as it unfolds, even when it is not going to our plan or schedule. Be prepared, and willing, to be flexible in order to keep moving in the right direction, whilst evaluating the consequences of not being on schedule, and making appropriate adjustments.

Remember that, when using Accounting behaviours, effective responses can come from any of the groups of Golden behaviours. Be alert to the potential of reacting to a situation with an ineffective behaviour. Also, an effective response may be generated by employing a number of different effective behaviours in combination.

An effective leader will recognise the importance of introducing the change or development process in a positive way, in order to get people on board, rather than generating confusion and uncertainty. At this stage, it is essential to demonstrate that we are Accounting for the uncertainty that accompanies a change process. Providing clear and detailed information about the parts of the process that you have worked through, such as timescale and process, will generate confidence in your leadership, and act to reduce the anxiety that uncertainty inevitably engenders in others. Providing structure will act against speculation being generated by the lack of clear information at the start of the process. Uncertainty increases the levels of speculation about how and when the changes are going to occur. Providing information about who will be leading the process, how employees will be involved in it and how they will be able to comment and contribute to it, will all support a positive change process.

When leading an organizational change process, I have always shared the major objectives and reasons with everyone affected by the change, whilst also keeping others in the organization aware of what's happening, before any overt actions have taken place. I have used written communications to provide a brief overview of the process, the reason for it and the overall major objectives. This has been followed by a range of meetings, open to all, to provide an opportunity to provide more detail, to answer questions about the process, and to invite collaboration and input into the process. These have generally occurred whilst working on producing a plan of action, so I have been comfortable in responding by saying that I don't have all of the answers, and inviting comments and suggestions.

Entering into a dialogue at an early stage not only demonstrates open communication channels, it also enables a check to be made on whether the underlying issues identified as the source of the organizational problems have been correctly, and fully, identified, before generating and rolling out the organizational development or change process.

Structuring

The key characteristics of Structuring behaviours are: inspiring, authoritative, helpful, firm, consistent, and well-organized.

When using these behaviours, it is important to be factual and honest. In any change process, leaders show authoritative behaviour by giving clear explanations to employees about why the organization needs to change (for example, a need to cut costs, improve customer satisfaction, or make changes needed to comply with new regulations). This is probably the most important piece of information to share with everyone affected by the change process. The explanation also helps relevant staff and teams to start thinking about the part they can play. Being honest about the probable consequences of not making the changes, and how that might adversely affect the organization and those in it, is also valuable information to share.

Leaders can be inspirational by communicating the positive outcomes following the changes, so that employees can start to see the advantages of making the changes, even before the process has started. This positive picture inspires contributions towards achieving it. However, being honest is also about demonstrating empathy and compassion for the challenges everyone may face, including yourself, and expressing your own feelings, while also being positive and assertive. Walk the talk!

Guiding and Directing people through change requires the change agent to be well-organized and consistent. Providing an indicative timescale and the key parts of the process, with a built-in contingency for the unexpected, will reduce uncertainty and anxiety, as well as reducing the potential of needing to reschedule the process when the unexpected happens, as it inevitably will, during any change process. Information about the people leading and supporting the process, along with explaining consultation and communication channels, as well as the mechanism for concerns to be aired and discussed with management, will also support building relationships and encourage good communications. Providing weekly or monthly updates on progress, and successes will help people to feel positive and well-informed.

Change leaders need to be firm and not backtrack. Being flexible is different, and useful! Making adjustments and taking a different course of action as other options emerge during the process is part of a successful change process. In any change process there will be some essential goals (non-negotiable, e.g. reducing production costs by x%, or overheads by y%, or relocating, or increasing profit margins by z%) as well as some aspects which will be grey areas (negotiable), and will be open to discussion and agreement; for example, where we might relocate to, how to achieve the reductions needed, and how to increase the profit margins. Being clear and firm about the non-negotiable parts, whilst being clear and flexible about the aspects that are undecided and negotiable with those affected, supports structural clarity of the process.

Being helpful and approachable will support open communication channels and build positive relationships. But do be careful about what constitutes being helpful! Being helpful does not include rescuing or taking on responsibilities that are not yours. Being helpful is about being supportive and providing advice, suggestions and options, as well as listening and inviting others to look for options and different courses of action that they can take. Making training available on creative problem-solving techniques could be helpful to support staff to work through problems that they encounter during the change process.

These behaviours are essential at the commencement of the process, to reduce the speculation that inevitably occurs if the structure and processes are unclear or vague. During the implementation period, providing information on what's happening helps enable employees to separate reality from speculation and rumours.

Case study

Ella was aware that there was likely to be speculation and rumours generated by the change process she and her senior colleagues were initiating in their organization. As well as sending out regular bulletins on progress, Ella arranged some open meetings and drop-in opportunities to enable employees to access more detail, and keep communication channels open so that it would become more of a shared process. This also provided regular opportunities for Ella and her colleagues to check out, and access information about, the concerns, rumours and speculations that were emerging alongside the change process. As well as providing some effective Structuring, this also provided opportunities for some effective Nurturing to take place, and encouraged Cooperative behaviours.

Nurturing

The key characteristics of Nurturing behaviours are: cherishing, accepting, understanding, compassionate, empathic, and encouraging.

An effective leader will listen! Listening, rather than merely hearing, enables us to be empathetic, compassionate, and accepting of the impact of the change process on those affected by it. The remaining Nurturing behaviours can then be used to understand what's affecting others, to cherish their contributions and their sharing and to encourage them, with support, to move forward in a positive way. These behaviours help leaders and change agents to be supportive and encouraging.

Everyone in an organization undergoing a change, or organizational development, process has options, and choices to make. In employing Nurturing behaviours, effective leaders can provide support to help employees to recognise and explore their options, and to make their own choices. Effective leaders should avoid slipping into ineffective behaviours such as advising other people which courses of action to take (Dominating behaviour). Effective behaviours would be being respectful and supportive of employees' autonomy to explore their options, and to choose and take the ones that are best for themselves. Providing support to help them to make the best decisions they can, and to carry them through is far more effective and supportive.

One of the most important things that effective leaders can do to support people through the change process is to acknowledge their situation. This provides an opportunity for leaders to empathise with them, to be compassionate and to focus on providing them with the support that they need; and this may be through referring them to someone else, rather than taking on that responsibility themselves, which would leave them in a pit that they would have difficulty climbing out of. It is important to stay focused on the task of managing the change process. It's also important to Nurture ourselves, as well as others. Slipping into Purple Pitfalls, such as over-committing ourselves and taking too much on, with the best intentions (of course!), will not help the process in the longer term.

As change managers, it can sometimes be difficult to understand the anxiety and concerns of some employees. After all, we are committed to achieving the change, for the benefit for everyone in the organization. We know why it is needed, as well as the consequences of not making the changes. Not all stakeholders, however, view the change or development process in the same way. For some, it can represent a major upheaval, with an inability to appreciate their role or function at the end of it. Some employees may need to reskill or change roles, to retrain or take on a completely different role or function, or even relocate to a different base, and this can represent a bridge too far for some. As an effective leader, it's important to be open to these possibilities, to understand and be accepting of their perspective. It's only when you can do this, that you can be truly supportive and Nurturing. Within this frame, it becomes easier to empathise with those employees that are significantly affected by the changes, and to support them, through positive conversations, to help them find the best solution for themselves.

Beware of moving into unhelpful Purple Pitfall behaviours, hoping to avoid conflict or having to make tough decisions, or even upsetting some people. Some people will not like the changes and development that is needed to keep organizations efficient, effective and profitable. Over-promising and giving unrealistic assurances, instead of being open, honest and accepting of the consequences of the needed changes is a common pitfall to make.

Case study

In one change process that I was involved in, the Managing Director, in an opening discussion with the management team, assured everyone present that there were no plans to reduce the number of departments and, therefore, the number of people on the management team. Except that, the organizational structure that we had developed, and agreed, included a merging of some departments with a consequent reduction in two positions on the management team. As part of the change process he offered voluntary redundancy packages to everyone, expecting two take-ups from within the management team, which didn't happen. His credibility ended at that point, and the change process became almost unmanageable.

Cooperative

The key characteristics of Cooperative behaviours are: confident, friendly, adaptable, assertive, considerate, and resilient.

Using these behaviours as change agents supports the objective of working *with* people in the organization to achieve the desired changes. Working cooperatively encourages, promotes and facilitates working together to identify the problems, to explore and seek options, to identify implications and to choose the most appropriate course of action. Leaders should be sharing and communicating their thoughts and feelings as part of the process, whilst respecting the decisions that have already been made, and the actions that have been taken to implement the change process.

Being confident, assertive and, at the same time, adaptable, instead of immovable, is a demonstration of potent leadership skills, and can be inspirational to others.

Change agents will have spent considerable time and energy identifying and understanding the issues and/or pressures that the organization is facing. Effective leaders will have gathered information, considered many options, and discussed them with others, before generating the best solution, and designing the change process to implement it. Consequently, those leading the change process can be confident and assertive, because they know why they are doing it, in the way they are doing it: they know the end goal and how to get there. But effective leaders acknowledge that they don't always know the best path! So they need to be flexible and adaptable, in order to negotiate and get around difficulties and unexpected obstacles that arise, and get in the way of achieving the goal. Knowing the end point, and staying *en route* to achieving it is a great strategy.

Sharing our knowledge and process, and explaining the rationale behind aspects of the changes can prove enlightening, as well as reassuring, for others. Sharing the other options that were considered and the reasons for not choosing them can also reduce, or even remove, resistance, as others begin to understand and appreciate the reasons for what's being done, in the way that it is being implemented. It invites others to Account for the knowledge, expertise and skills needed to effectively manage a change process.

Listening to concerns and potential obstacles, being considerate and prepared to adjust the process and schedule in order to maintain progress, through co-operating with others in order to stay on track, helps to find the most effective path through the change process. Deviations are fine, so long as getting back on track without a major hold-up is achieved. Time can be a useful lubricant, providing opportunities for a change in the culture, or frames of reference, to occur. Staying, stubbornly, with the plans generated in the first place is a Purple Pitfall (resistant), as it can increase the resistance to the change, resulting in minimal progress being achieved whilst the re-sistance is addressed. Cooperating to find a solution together is a better option: it may not be ideal, but if it generates progress, it's better than being in a traffic jam.

Being friendly is different to being a friend! It's important to have good relationships with others to be able to communicate well, and openly. Being cooperative means being alongside (or "with") others that we are transacting with. Being dismissive of their perspectives or concerns, or being overly submissive are Purple Pitfalls to be on the lookout for, and avoided. Acknowledging and Accounting for the difficult processes that are taking place, and their potential impact on the people in the organization, whilst treating everyone with respect, will support and engender cooperation and lubricate the change process.

Finally, and probably most importantly for leaders and change agents, is the need to be resilient! Change is not an easy process to lead or to manage and it isn't possible to make everyone happy, or to solve all of the problems that come with an organizational development or change process. Some people will not like the proposed changes, or the impact of the changes on themselves. Being flexible and adaptable, whilst also being understanding, considerate and empathetic, and still continuing to make progress, should be the goal of the effective leader.

Being cooperative means that leaders also need to be cooperative, as well as expecting others to be cooperative. It's not a one way street!

Case study

I recall one organisational change process where we had decided on a new structure to take forward, when an employee pointed out what they felt was a flaw in our proposals. We listened, sought further information from them about the flaw that they perceived, and asked them for their solution. They had been working on a governmental regulatory review which would result, imminently, in the transferring of some current services to a new centralised regulatory body, which meant that we would no longer be responsible for the delivery of the service. So we adjusted the structure to take account of their forward thinking, and avoided the difficulties that we would otherwise have encountered.

Spontaneous

The key characteristics of Spontaneous behaviours are: creative, curious, zestful, imaginative, expressive, and playful.

Using Spontaneous behaviour means being free to choose from all available options, not just the ones that we feel comfortable with. It doesn't mean that decisions need to be made quickly or "in the moment"! It does, however, mean not being constrained by cultural expectations or past experiences.

The best solutions are a consequence of good information gathering and processing, and generating a range of possible solutions. It's problem solving with the information that we get from our Accounting behaviours. A Purple Pitfall here can be disastrous! Being unorganised, hurried, egocentric, and inconsiderate can result in inadequate information and data being gathered, only considering a limited range of solutions, and looking for a quick fix.

Taking adequate time to gather information and analyse the data will be time well spent. Properly exploring possibilities may uncover, or reveal, the best solutions. This is where accessing your curiosity can be extremely helpful. Be curious about what's happening, why it's happening and how it's happening, as well as what's missing, what information you don't have, and what options you are not seeing. Be curious about your own feelings and how they might be influencing you. Be curious about how others are feeling and how that might be affecting their thinking, behaviour, and actions. Be curious about the future and use that curiosity to work out the likely implications of your options, and feed those into your decision making processes.

Being imaginative here can help: what if ...? How might that work? How might you check that out? Can you imagine what it will be like when the development/change process has been completed? Can you leave the constraints behind and ask yourself questions like "what do I really need?" "What resource or support would I like to have if I could have what I wanted?" "Who would I like to be working with?"

Here's another beckoning opportunity to fall into a Purple pit! Beware of becoming over-enthusiastic to get going, setting the change process in motion, and forgetting to properly engage with your creative processes. When we're being creative, we can access and use our intuition, skills, competencies, and experiences; and in solving problems we can Account for our past successes (and failures!). Accessing the resources of others in order to make good decisions, helps to check out whether or not something has been missed.

Having made some good decisions, it's time to communicate them through being expressive - about what you are passionate about, about what's exciting you and what might still be concerning you. Sharing your thoughts, feelings, and processes are all part of being Spontaneous. And sharing your past experiences of organizational development and change processes with those around you, who may wish to learn from you, can support improving relationships, and maintaining good communication channels. It's okay to be zestful – full of energy and enthusiasm - and encourage others to be part of what you're doing and to share in your successes.

And it's also okay to be playful! Really! Be passionate about what you are passionate about. You can share your excitement, and show it. And you can enjoy what you're doing and celebrate your successes along the way. You can be yourself.

Case study

In one organizational change process, we decided to be playful with white chocolate mice. We left them as token rewards on the desks of employees who were positively supporting the change process by inputting ideas and/or making positive suggestions and/or comments on our proposals, and also for completion of tasks in the process. We didn't announce this, we just did it. It soon became part of the organization's culture, and the white chocolate mice became sought after items.

Putting it all together

What I've covered so far is how functionally fluent behaviours can support good communications and engender good, positive and supportive relationships within an organizational setting related, more specifically, to the processes needed in an organizational change process. I said earlier that organizational change is a process that has common elements in it, and that functional fluency can support the whole of that process. What I want to do now is provide some details of a generic transformational change process that can provide a framework for organizational change, look at another model that can help remaining functionally fluent, and then show how these all fit together in practice, through a case study of an actual change process.

Mezirow's transformational learning and change process

Mezirow's transformational learning and change process provides a structure that can be used as a base for an organizational change process. I referred earlier to the disorientating dilemma that is at the start of the change process. I usually refer to this as a disconcerting dilemma – a situation which generates confusion and uncertainty, and a feeling of indecision and stuckness. In these circumstances, we usually choose to follow what we did the last time we were in this position, or in a similar situation in the past, and we would be falling into Purple Pitfall behaviours. We know how that worked out, and we coped with it, so it is familiar, even if some parts were unpleasant, but predictable – or so we believe. Except that, in an organizational development/change process, little, if anything, is predictable. Each organization is different, the leaders and managers are different, what organizations do is different, and the culture of each organization is unique. So, choosing to follow a previous pattern in the expectation that we will be in control of what will happen, is pretty delusional.

Mezirow's process recognises that transformational learning is an essential part of, and is a necessary precursor to, transformational change. "Transformation" requires something significant to change. That is, something "old" is replaced with something "new". It means that a change in our frame of reference has occurred. An example might be when typewriters were replaced with word processors, or handwritten financial accounts and ledgers were replaced by spreadsheets and accounting software packages.

His process is a formula to help us stay in touch with reality to support making present-centred decisions. The steps in the process support Accounting behaviours through the gathering of factual information that we can access from a range of sources (including internal thoughts, feelings, and processes). Evaluating the data that we have to hand at each stage, and considering a range of options and their implications, support good decision making. Then taking time to work out what we need, to be in a position to implement it, before setting out on the journey, brings into play the positive behaviours from the other parts of the Functional Fluency model, to generate a positive outcome. Of course, at the end of an organizational change process "old" structures, processes and culture have been replaced with "new" ones. So the organization is different, due mostly to the learning that has taken place through the process, about how to do things differently.

His 10 stages support the learning and change process to succeed:

1 A disorienting dilemma.
2 Self-examination with feelings of fear, anger, guilt, or shame.
3 A critical assessment of assumptions.
4 Recognition that one's discontent and the process of transformation are shared.
5 Exploration of options for new roles, relationships, and actions.
6 Planning a course of action.
7 Acquiring knowledge and skills for implementing one's plans.
8 Provisional trying of new roles.
9 Building competence and self-confidence in new roles and relationships.
10 A reintegration into one's life on the basis of conditions dictated by one's new perspectives

As we work through the case study, the stages will become apparent.

Co-creative Transactional Analysis (CCTA)

Functional Fluency has its origins in Transactional Analysis – a positive psychology developed by Eric Berne in the 1950s and 60s. Not surprisingly, Co-creative Transactional Analysis, a comparatively recent development of Berne's theory, works well with Functional Fluency to support using effective behaviours, and avoiding unhelpful ones. The model was developed in 2000, by Graeme Summers and Keith Tudor[2], as a means of supporting present-centred processing, and working in relationship to explore and find solutions to problems, which is exactly what Functional Fluency supports, so they go hand in hand.

There are four basic tenets:

We-ness: working together and pooling resources helps to explore issues and find better solutions to problems. This supports noticing things that, working alone, might have been missed (cooperative behaviours). Similarly, combining experiences and resources generates more solutions, and the identification of more implications than working alone, so that we are able to make more appropriate choices (Spontaneous behaviours). So, there will be more options to consider and choose from (Accounting behaviours): and, when we've made a decision, there will be two or more of us to action it.

Examples of this principle would be offering to share our solution to a similar problem that we had successfully negotiated in the past, or offering to take on a role that we are good at, or offering to provide training for others in a skill or process that we are very competent in.

Shared responsibility: no one person can be totally responsible for the success of an organizational change process. Sharing the responsibility for defining the issue, considering options and finding a solution, and for the success of implementing the programme (Cooperative behaviours) is helpful and supportive. There are times when each person can take more responsibility for some aspect of the work, which means that each of us can contribute our strengths and experiences when it's most appropriate. We are not in competition – we are working together to achieve our shared goal.

> An example of this might be stepping up to take some responsibility for a project, or offering to support someone else to deliver a project or task, or stepping down and supporting someone else to take on a project that would provide a development opportunity for them, and offering our support to work alongside them.

Present centredness: this is particularly about staying in Accounting behaviours, accessing and using all of the attributes associated with it to keep us grounded in reality. We need to be alert to past feelings that are unduly influencing us, and explore them, in order to check out their validity (checking that we are not using Purple Pitfall behaviours). What are the fantasies that we are projecting onto the situation, that have no basis of reality in them? It also helps us to be grounded in reality when we are checking information that we have, exploring possible solutions, and projecting forward the resources and time that we need to complete the change process (checking that we are not using Marshmallowing behaviours). It's also about sharing and communicating our thoughts and feelings with those around us, in an honest way, and acknowledging and Accounting for our uncertainties and fears about the changes.

> An example of this would be voicing our vulnerability and/or concerns about the process and proposals, and/or bringing into the discussions any opportunities and/or threats that we identify, rather than assuming that others have already identified them.

Mutual positive regard: this (added by Robinson in 2020[3]) is about treating others (and ourselves) with positive regard. Not seeking to be better than others (Dominating behaviour), or to defer to them (Marshmallowing or submissive behaviours), but recognising and Accounting for the positive aspects of ourselves and others from an "I'm OK/you're OK"[4] perspective. It helps us to stay positive and grounded, and not to fantasise about things when they seem not to be going to plan: things just don't always go to plan! We don't need to blame ourselves or someone else! It may not be our fault, nor someone else being obstructive or purposely omitting to do something. Stay present centred, be curious and explore. Stay OK! Overall it's about treating ourselves and those around us with respect and working with others with positive intent (Cooperative behaviours).

> Examples of this would include not taking so much on, ourselves, that it becomes impossible to deliver our tasks/projects/roles, or offering our experience and competence to support someone else to learn a new skill or to take on a new role or task. Not expecting too much of others would also fall within this principle.

These principles support functionally fluent (helpful) behaviours. Equally, functionally fluent behaviours support staying within the CCTA framework. If you want to know more about this model, there are references at the end of this chapter.

Functional Fluency, Co-Creative Transactional Analysis and Mezirow's process complement and support each other because at the heart of each of them is the concept of being present-centred, and choosing appropriate actions and behaviours. Also, they all involve being in positive and supportive relationships with those around us.

Putting it into practice: a case study

As a practical example of how this can all come together, and how Functional Fluency can provide a constant support mechanism to organizational change processes, I'll relate how Functional Fluency supported an organizational change process that I led some years ago in an organization of around 1,200 employees, delivering a range of services at many different sites.

As you read through this case study, see if you can identify the functionally fluent behaviours that we (as a change management team) used to support the process – make some notes so that you can reflect on them at the end. I'll identify some of the main ones as I relate the story.

First, the disorienting dilemma: I was asked to lead an organization-wide change process to reduce net expenditure by around 10% within 12 months, ideally without reducing the services being delivered, and without increasing their cost by more than inflation rate. I was given four months to get to the implementation stage. Not an easy task in such a short time frame. Could I do it? It felt scary and confusing. Where would I start? Using Accounting behaviours enabled me to stay grounded and face the dilemma, including working through stage 2 of the process – exploring and accounting for the scary and confusing feelings being generated by facing the dilemma. These (Accounting) behaviours enabled me to gather relevant information, evaluate the task and quantify just what the numbers were. I quickly recognized I couldn't do it alone, and so I gathered a small team of four people, with particular skills (finance, administration, interpersonal skills, and experience of change processes) to work with me to achieve the change. We stayed present-centred and explored our task together. We focussed on the achievement of the objective. Spontaneous behaviours helped us to generate options; Structuring behaviours generated communications to the people in the organization, and Nurturing behaviours enabled us to be empathic and compassionate, whilst also acknowledging the difficulties we all might face in achieving the objective. We invited Cooperative behaviours by arranging meetings with managers and employees to explain our dilemma, and inviting comments and suggestions. We also put in place some training sessions for managers to help them to look for ways in which they might reduce their costs and/or increase their income. Being rational and grounded enabled us to see that increasing income for the same level of provision of services would, in effect, contribute to reducing net expenditure.

We weren't the only ones facing this dilemma – the other managers and employees were as well. So part of our job was to help them to face it too, and to work through the transformational process with them. We were already well into the process before we began to properly engage with the managers. We had to look at options and evaluate them, before we began to engage with the people in the organisation, albeit that we didn't know all of the answers, but we had decided on a process that we could take forward, and we could be flexible as we took it forward.

Some of the fear and anger surfaced in some of the meetings, but we reassured managers and staff that we would not be dictating to them how to make the savings, and that it would be an open and transparent process that they would be invited to fully engage with. It wasn't easy being confronted by some managers and staff telling us that it simply wasn't possible to achieve the required level of savings without cutting staff and services, especially when we didn't know it was possible, and being pressurised to provide information about redundancy packages that would be on offer. I took a risk here to admit that we didn't have all of the answers, and that we couldn't make any promises about redundancies or not cutting some services back. What I did do was give an assurance that we would work with the managers and teams to explore possibilities with them. We explained that our intention was to achieve the objective without making any cutbacks in services or personnel, and that their input was key to achieving this; after all, they knew their services better than we did.

Although we continued to be invited to react, and give information and assurances that we couldn't give, we resisted and reinforced our invitation and intent to work with everyone to achieve the objective. We did also provide some Structuring and Accounting by advising that we would, if the need arose, review individual services ourselves, in which case they would have less input to the decision making process. So we had been moving quickly through Mezirow's process, using helpful behaviours to keep ourselves on track.

As part of the organizational development process, we organized and delivered some training on the Functional Fluency model to support better communications within the organization as a whole. This was offered for teams to attend together, as well as for individuals to attend with employees from other teams. The latter had the best impact on the organization, as it provided an opportunity for direct communication between employees in different teams and locations, which enabled employees to interact directly with those in other teams and get a new perspective on the services or parts of a service that they were delivering. This programme, in particular, helped to challenge the cultural perception that change had to be painful. It provided an opportunity for employees to experience something different – support and encouragement (Nurturing). It also helped to build a more positive relationship with management and leaders.

Reflection

Take a little time out here to explore what might be the benefits of facilitating an understanding of the Functional Fluency model. How do you think that it might have improved communications within the organization? Make some notes about what you might expect the benefits to have been before you read on.

What we found was that employees began to speak directly to their colleagues more often. Numbers of e-mail communications reduced, and there was an unexpected rise in demand for meeting rooms. Employees reported feeling more valued and empowered, and less anxious about the impending change process.

We decided, as the core element of stage 3 (a critical assessment of assumptions), to invite all services to generate three options for the continuance of their service at a reduced "net" cost of 5, 10 and 15%. This invited the facility to explore the options of reducing costs, increasing income, or a mixture of the two. In particular, its purpose was to challenge the assumption that the current service delivery method and costs were the right ones and that it couldn't be done more efficiently and effectively, or differently! The 15% option really pushed the boundaries into challenging why the service was being provided at all! This process was also at the heart of Functional Fluency: Accounting for what *needed* to be delivered, rather than what *was* being delivered invited awareness, evaluation, enquiring, and rational behaviours, whilst remaining present centred. We provided financial information and support for their process by being available to work with them, and to provide advice and further information if required. We also provided models and resource to support evaluation of options.

In this stage we were providing Structure and being Nurturing whilst also encouraging Spontaneous and Cooperative behaviours (can you identify these behaviours from the above?). We invited we-ness whilst providing direction (Structure) and encouraging innovation (Nurturing and Spontaneous behaviours), and we supported shared responsibility by offering support and choice to managers and their teams to explore their services and to identify options for reducing their costs and/or increasing their income. In becoming advisers and sounding boards for their explorations, we used and invited mutual positive regard, whilst sharing with them the responsibility of finding solutions. In making our experience and knowledge available to them, we further invited we-ness (Cooperative behaviour) and were available to support present-centred processing (Accounting) as options were being evaluated.

We did provide a time structure for the process, with some waypoints that we were expecting to be met, albeit with some flexibility, and we invited discussions about the waypoints, which we were comfortable to move around by discussion and agreement, as long as the end point was kept in mind.

Reflection

Take some more time out here to consider what responses you think that we might have had to this "hands off" approach? Also, reflect on what other helpful behaviours you saw us using so far.

Generally, we had a good response. There was some initial confusion because the managers and staff were still expecting us to go in and tell them what should be cut back so that they could then work out the consequences and start a dialogue around why they couldn't do it. We had been particularly careful to avoid this potential scenario by not engaging in unhelpful Dominating behaviours (bossy, knows better and fault finding), which reduced the potential of generating Compliant/Resistant responses (defiant, rebellious and submissive).

We initially worked with a handful of teams to help them to explore their options, and then we arranged some group meetings across the organization where these managers and team leaders could share what they had come up with. This process began to address the fourth stage in the process: a recognition that the resistance and discontent was just getting in the way of getting on with the task, and that where there had been some cooperation (shared responsibility) and working together (we-ness), there was significant success, and the outcomes were not particularly painful. The managers that we had worked with explained the process that they had gone through, the support that they had accessed and where they had got to. There was still some further work to do to fine tune their options and to explore the possibilities that had emerged during the process, but they were 75% through the process. Generally, the managers/team leaders went away both empowered and motivated to get on with the task.

During this process, we focused on being helpful to, and adaptable with, the managers that were engaging with us. We were understanding and compassionate with those managers that were finding the task difficult, and we were considerate of the challenges they were facing, whilst remaining assertive about completion of the task and inviting co-operation with our team and the managers that had already gone through the process with us. We invited creative solutions to be found to difficult issues through a process of inviting them to explain the difficulties to us and working with them to generate possible solutions. This was now addressing the fifth stage of the process (exploring new roles and relationships, and actions) and moving into the sixth stage (planning a course of action). Of course, some of the managers had already gone through these stages with us, but it was now organization-wide and everyone was in the process of planning a course of action, or moving into stage seven (acquiring knowledge and skills to implement the action plan).

Reflection

Can you identify the helpful behaviours that we had been using in this important stage of the process? Make a list of the ones that you can see might have been being employed.

Through providing help and assistance, we supported the managers to complete their initial task – that of identifying options and costing them out. What we then had to do was to support the managers to implement them.

We sat down with each of the managers and explored the options that they had generated, and we agreed with each of them which of the options they were going to implement. So they now had a basic plan of action (stage 6) and as we were now moving into stage 7, we invited them to identify, what resources they needed to get on with the implementation. Was there any new knowledge and/or skills they needed, or access to support or external resource? We provided support to them in implementing their plans, so that they grew into their new role and gained confidence in their ability to transform their own service (stages 8 and 9).

This process became an annual event, going on in the background during the generation of, and updating, the organization's business plan and the production of the annual budget (stage 10).

What we found was a different level of engagement with managers and employees. The organizational culture changed significantly with much more openness and improved communication.

Maybe you're wondering whether we actually achieved the objective of reducing costs by 10%? What was achieved was around a 12% overall reduction in net costs (made up of a mixture of reduced expenditure and increased income) without any significant effect on the services delivered. In addition, there were no redundancies needed, and we also saw an increase in customer satisfaction.

I hope that you can see how Functional Fluency supported the organization change process within this example. It pervaded our interactions with managers and staff throughout the change process. The time and resource allocated to the early workshop sessions to introduce employees to the Functional Fluency model enabled and facilitated a significant change in perspective throughout the organization, which supported far more open and less defensive conversations with managers and teams about the task that they were invited into with us: to achieve the organization's goal of reducing overall costs. Mezirow's process is a helpful model to use for the whole process, as it ensures that important stages are not overlooked and/or bypassed. The Co-creative TA aspects support the building of positive, open relationships, where we can work together, sharing resources and ideas to generate better solutions than if we were working separately, with the added bonus that it establishes better working relationships that carry on into the future. The functionally fluent behaviours, employed throughout the process, significantly helped and supported clearer communications and the building of healthier relationships, as well as a change of culture in the organization.

Summary

Functionally fluent organizational development and change leaders:

- Focus on staying grounded and aware of what's actually taking place, so that they can account for it effectively.
- Build open and non-defensive relationships with the people that they engage with.
- Consciously avoid reacting to pressure and take time to respond with an effective behaviour or a combination of effective behaviours.
- Use Accounting and Spontaneous behaviours effectively in tandem to plan ahead, with contingency options built in.
- Invite helpful behaviours in others by sharing the responsibility and inviting (and responding positively to) Cooperative behaviours.
- Treat others with respect and positive regard, so avoiding Dominating and Marshmallowing behaviours and reducing the potential of Compliant/Resistant or Immature behavioural responses from others.
- Are comfortable sharing their thoughts and feelings with others.
- Are confident, considerate and resilient, whilst also being flexible and focused on the longer term objectives.

Notes

1 Mezirow, J. & Associates (2000) *Learning as Transformation*. San Francisco: Jossey-Bass.
2 Summers, G. & Tudor, K. "Co-creative Transactional Analysis". *Transactional Analysis Journal*, 30:1. 2000.
3 Robinson, P. "Co-creative Transformational Learning as a way to break out of Script". *Transactional Analysis Journal* 50:1. 2020.
4 Eric Berne used this shorthand to describe how our behaviour is influenced, at a non-conscious psychological level, when we interact with others. There are 2 existential life positions: "OK" or "not OK". When we interact with others, we each have these two "options", so there are 4 possible ways of interacting: I'm OK, you're not OK; I'm not OK, you're not OK; I'm not OK, you're OK and I'm OK, you're OK. For more information see, for example: Berne, E. (1964) *Games People Play*. Harmondsworth: Penguin books; Harris, T. A. (1973) *I'm OK - You're OK*. London: Pan Books.

Appendix

Further information, learning and training in Functional Fluency is available from Functional Fluency International at functionalfluency.com and is available to anyone. It is free to download a Starter Pack with explanations of the model and its use, and Discovery Membership is available to anyone interested in learning more about Functional Fluency for themselves or others. This gives you access to online courses and resources.

Training programmes for anyone interested are provided throughout the year.

The TIFF Profile

It is recommended that one of the best ways to learn more about using Functional Fluency is to have a personal profile – Temple Index of Functional Fluency (TIFF). Many of the people in the case studies in this book had undertaken a TIFF profile with a coach. This is a metric which has been fully researched by Dr. Susannah Temple. As it is about behaviour rather than personality, it can more easily be used as a developmental tool to identify strengths, and make changes to ineffective behaviour which drains energy. The profile consists of a questionnaire, the results of which are discussed with a licensed TIFF provider in one or two coaching sessions. TIFF does not label you in any way, but the TIFF provider will help you to gain the learning which is specifically relevant to you in the session so that you can find out which effective behaviours you are already using, and how to exchange your Purple Pitfalls for the Golden Five.

To get your TIFF profile, go to TIFF the People Development Tool (https://functionalfluency.com/about/functional-fluency/tiff-the-people-development-tool) for more information and a link to TIFF Providers around the world, or go straight to TIFF Providers (https://functionalfluency.com/people/tiff-providers) where you can choose a provider who is either close to you for an in-person session, or who will provide your profiling session face-to-face online.

Many of the TIFF Providers can also offer training in Functional Fluency to groups, and tailored to organizational or team needs. All the authors of this book are TIFF providers, so you can contact them through the website.

If you are a coach or trainer, and would like to become licensed to provide TIFF profiles to your clients or organization, go to TIFF Provider Licensing Training and/or contact info@functionalfluency.com, (https://functionalflu ency.com/training-programs/6/tiff-provider-licensing-training).

Index